Pedagogy for Conceptual Thinking and Meaning Equivalence:

Emerging Research and Opportunities

Masha Etkind
Ryerson University, Canada

Uri Shafrir
University of Toronto, Canada

A volume in the Advances in Educational Technologies and Instructional Design (AETID) Book Series

Published in the United States of America by
IGI Global
Information Science Reference (an imprint of IGI Global)
701 E. Chocolate Avenue
Hershey PA, USA 17033
Tel: 717-533-8845
Fax: 717-533-8661
E-mail: cust@igi-global.com
Web site: http://www.igi-global.com

Copyright © 2020 by IGI Global. All rights reserved. No part of this publication may be reproduced, stored or distributed in any form or by any means, electronic or mechanical, including photocopying, without written permission from the publisher.
Product or company names used in this set are for identification purposes only. Inclusion of the names of the products or companies does not indicate a claim of ownership by IGI Global of the trademark or registered trademark.

Library of Congress Cataloging-in-Publication Data

Names: Etkind, Masha, 1946- editor. | Shafrir, Uri, editor.
Title: Pedagogy for conceptual thinking and meaning equivalence : emerging
   research and opportunities / Masha Etkind and Uri Shafrir, editors.
Description: Hershey, PA : Information Science Reference, 2020. | Includes
   bibliographical references and index. | Summary: "This book explores
   enhancing learning outcomes with pedagogy for conceptual thinking and
   meaning equivalent reusable learning objects"-- Provided by publisher.
Identifiers: LCCN 2019035511 (print) | LCCN 2019035512 (ebook) | ISBN
   9781799819851 (hardcover) | ISBN 9781799819868 (paperback) | ISBN
   9781799819875 (ebook)
Subjects: LCSH: Concept learning.
Classification: LCC LB1062 .P363 2020 (print) | LCC LB1062 (ebook) | DDC
   370.15/23--dc23
LC record available at https://lccn.loc.gov/2019035511
LC ebook record available at https://lccn.loc.gov/2019035512

British Cataloguing in Publication Data
A Cataloguing in Publication record for this book is available from the British Library.

All work contributed to this book is new, previously-unpublished material.
The views expressed in this book are those of the authors, but not necessarily of the publisher.

For electronic access to this publication, please contact: eresources@igi-global.com.

Advances in Educational Technologies and Instructional Design (AETID) Book Series

ISSN:2326-8905
EISSN:2326-8913

Editor-in-Chief: Lawrence A. Tomei, Robert Morris University, USA

MISSION

Education has undergone, and continues to undergo, immense changes in the way it is enacted and distributed to both child and adult learners. In modern education, the traditional classroom learning experience has evolved to include technological resources and to provide online classroom opportunities to students of all ages regardless of their geographical locations. From distance education, Massive-Open-Online-Courses (MOOCs), and electronic tablets in the classroom, technology is now an integral part of learning and is also affecting the way educators communicate information to students.

The **Advances in Educational Technologies & Instructional Design (AETID) Book Series** explores new research and theories for facilitating learning and improving educational performance utilizing technological processes and resources. The series examines technologies that can be integrated into K-12 classrooms to improve skills and learning abilities in all subjects including STEM education and language learning. Additionally, it studies the emergence of fully online classrooms for young and adult learners alike, and the communication and accountability challenges that can arise. Trending topics that are covered include adaptive learning, game-based learning, virtual school environments, and social media effects. School administrators, educators, academicians, researchers, and students will find this series to be an excellent resource for the effective design and implementation of learning technologies in their classes.

COVERAGE

- Collaboration Tools
- Higher Education Technologies
- Social Media Effects on Education
- Online Media in Classrooms
- Curriculum Development
- K-12 Educational Technologies
- Adaptive Learning
- Digital Divide in Education
- Classroom Response Systems
- Instructional Design Models

IGI Global is currently accepting manuscripts for publication within this series. To submit a proposal for a volume in this series, please contact our Acquisition Editors at Acquisitions@igi-global.com or visit: http://www.igi-global.com/publish/.

The Advances in Educational Technologies and Instructional Design (AETID) Book Series (ISSN 2326-8905) is published by IGI Global, 701 E. Chocolate Avenue, Hershey, PA 17033-1240, USA, www.igi-global.com. This series is composed of titles available for purchase individually; each title is edited to be contextually exclusive from any other title within the series. For pricing and ordering information please visit http://www.igi-global.com/book-series/advances-educational-technologies-instructional-design/73678. Postmaster: Send all address changes to above address. ©© 2020 IGI Global. All rights, including translation in other languages reserved by the publisher. No part of this series may be reproduced or used in any form or by any means – graphics, electronic, or mechanical, including photocopying, recording, taping, or information and retrieval systems – without written permission from the publisher, except for non commercial, educational use, including classroom teaching purposes. The views expressed in this series are those of the authors, but not necessarily of IGI Global.

Titles in this Series

For a list of additional titles in this series, please visit:
https://www.igi-global.com/book-series/advances-educational-technologies-instructional-design/73678

Form, Function, and Style in Instructional Design Emerging Research and Opportunities
Shalin Hai-Jew (Kansas State University, USA)
Information Science Reference • ©2020 • 203pp • H/C (ISBN: 9781522598336) • US $155.00

The Roles of Technology and Globalization in Educational Transformation
Blessing F. Adeoye (Walden University, USA) and Gladys Arome (Marian University, USA)
Information Science Reference • ©2020 • 259pp • H/C (ISBN: 9781522597469) • US $195.00

Utilizing Educational Data Mining Techniques for Improved Learning Emerging Research and Opportunities
Chintan Bhatt (Charotar University of Science and Technology, India) Priti Srinivas Sajja (Sardar Patel University, India) and Sidath Liyanage (University of Kelaniya, Sri Lanka)
Information Science Reference • ©2020 • 166pp • H/C (ISBN: 9781799800101) • US $165.00

Claiming Identity Through Redefined Teaching in Construction Programs
Sherif Mostafa (Griffith University, Australia) and Payam Rahnamayiezekavat (Western Sydney University, Australia)
Information Science Reference • ©2020 • 259pp • H/C (ISBN: 9781522584520) • US $185.00

Global Perspectives on Teaching and Learning Paths in Islamic Education
Miftachul Huda (Universiti Pendidikan Sultan Idris Malaysia, Malaysia) Jimaain Safar (Universiti Teknologi Malaysia, Malaysia) Ahmad Kilani Mohamed (Universiti Teknologi Malaysia, Malaysia) Kamarul Azmi Jasmi (Universiti Teknologi Malaysia, Malaysia) and Bushrah Basiron (Universiti Teknologi Malaysia, Malaysia)
Information Science Reference • ©2020 • 341pp • H/C (ISBN: 9781522585282) • US $195.00

Social Justice and Putting Theory Into Practice in Schools and Communities
Susan Trostle Brand (University of Rhode Island, USA) and Lori E. Ciccomascolo (University of Rhode Island, USA)
Information Science Reference • ©2020 • 359pp • H/C (ISBN: 9781522594345) • US $195.00

For an entire list of titles in this series, please visit:
https://www.igi-global.com/book-series/advances-educational-technologies-instructional-design/73678

701 East Chocolate Avenue, Hershey, PA 17033, USA
Tel: 717-533-8845 x100 • Fax: 717-533-8661
E-Mail: cust@igi-global.com • www.igi-global.com

Table of Contents

Preface vii

Chapter 1
High Order of Conceptual Thinking: Find the Equivalence of Meaning 1
    Masha Etkind, Ryerson University, Canada

Chapter 2
Meaning Equivalence Reusable Learning Objects (MERLO) Access
to Knowledge in Early Digital Era and Development of Pedagogy for
Conceptual Thinking 22
    Uri Shafrir, University of Toronto, Canada

Chapter 3
Enhancing Conceptual Thinking With Interactive Concept Discovery
(INCOD) 54
    Masha Etkinda, Ryerson University, Toronto, Canada
    Uri Shafrir, University of Toronto, Canada

Chapter 4
Teachers Involved in Designing MERLO Items 61
    Ornella Robutti, Università di Torino, Italy
    Paola Carante, Università di Torino, Italy
    Theodosia Prodromou, University of New England, Australia
    Ron S. Kenett, The KPA Group and the Samuel Neaman Institute,
        Technion, Israel

Chapter 5
Production of Evidence-Based Informed Consent (EBIC) With Meaning Equivalence Reusable Learning Objects (MERLO): An Application on the Clinical Setting..86
    Myrtha Elvia Reyna Vargas, University of Toronto, Canada
    Wendy Lou, University of Toronto, Canada
    Ron S. Kenett, Technion Israel, Israel

Chapter 6
Using Concept Maps With Errors to Identify Misconceptions: The Role of Instructional Design to Create Large-Scale On-Line Solutions........................117
    Paulo Rogério Miranda Correia, University of São Paulo, Brazil
    Joana Aguiar, University of São Paulo, Brazil
    Brian Moon, Perigean Technologies, USA

Related Readings 135

About the Contributors 150

Index 153

Preface

EQUIVALENCE OF MEANING

In many situations in our daily life we feel the need to express the same meaning by repeating a discourse. This need seems not to be content or discourse-specific, and to apply to different types of discourse - descriptive, abstract, narrative and expository. For example, we repeat a narrative discourse when we 'tell the same story all over again', maybe to a different person. We sometime repeat an expository discourse as when we give a 'repeat-performance' of a lecture on a specific topic to parallel sections of a class; or when we have to reconstruct a lost paragraph that has not been saved in time to avoid the calamity of a computer crash. On other occasions we find it spontaneously convenient to repeat a sentence that re-defines a complex concept in the course of a conversation.

What is the meaning of "repeat" in such circumstances? Does it mean that the second (third, fourth, etc.) repetition is identical – equal in all details – to the first discourse? Surely not. What we mean by 'repeat-performance' is not the verbatim quote of the original discourse but its re-representation - the re-construction and re-transmission of meaning. Such re-construction is often prompted by a dynamic relationship within which meaning is being constructed, develops and often also constrained. In contrast to classic semiotic theory that anchors meaning in the link between signified and signifier, i.e. the text, Gergen (1994) posits relationship at the fulcrum of meaning construction: Meaning is bestowed on an utterance by the relationship between speaker and listener, a relationship that is subject to dynamic supplements that often act to change the utterance or the text, while refining the equivalence-of-meaning (Evans, 2006; Kintch & Mangalath, 2011). The addition of an incorporeal component to the corporeal signifier/signified doublet has roots that go back over 2000 years. The Stoics called it *lekton*: "It is the thing meant by a speaker by successfully expressing a thought, as well as the thing understood by the one who comprehends the expression" (Smith, 1997, p. 26). Along the same line of reasoning, Uspensky (1962/1977) invoked Shannon's Theory of Information

(1948) to define meaning in the context of the Semiotics of Art: "Meaning can be understood as a series of associations and ideas that are linked to a symbol and is generally defined as the invariant in reversible operations of translation" (p. 171; see: Ellerman, 2009).

While we may often feel that in subsequent representations we expressed 'the same' meaning as in the original discourse, it is easy to verify that, in fact, while conserving the meaning encoded in the original discourse, in subsequent representations we expressed it in different ways. We do so by paraphrasing, putting things 'in other words'; by choice of metaphor; and by changing emphasis, point-of-view, discourse style, etc. Thus the original representation looks (or sounds) different from the second representation of the meaning; which looks/sounds still different than a third representation; etc. We offer the term *meaning equivalence* to designate this commonality of meaning, *the meaning conserved across several such representations*. In psychological terms we operationalize the set-theoretic definition of meaning equivalence as the ability to transcode equivalence-of-meaning through multiple representations within and across sign systems. Meaning equivalence may be defined in set-theoretical terms as a polymorphous - one-to-many - transformation of meaning within a sign system or across sign systems.

A review of the literature reveals that our ability to express meaning effortlessly in a multitude of ways has long been recognized by philosophers, linguists, semioticians, mathematicians, scientists, psychologists, and educators as playing an enabling role in human and cultural development. In his seminal work on multiple representations and human potential, the Russian semiotician Ivanov (1965/1977) expressed this role clearly: "A human individual's potential can be evaluated by describing all the sign systems he can use, including both multilevel sign systems composed of natural and scientific languages and mono-level sign systems such as the natural languages" (p. 32).

Experience tells us that conveying equivalence-of-meaning across several different utterances is unremarkable, and that it is more the rule than the exception. If so, there must be something about natural language that makes it possible. Indeed, some linguists and semioticians conferred definitional status on equivalence-of-meaning as an essential descriptor of natural language. Ivanov (1976) described the work of the Russian mathematician Kolmogorov on structural analysis of natural languages. According to Ivanov (1976), Kolmogorov viewed the writer's work, linguistically speaking, as the process of selecting a single text that satisfies a set of esthetical criteria out of a pool of possible phrases that transmits a content, which encodes a meaning residing in the writer's mind. This is possible because of a specific characteristic of natural language, which allows it to express identical meaning through different grammatical compositions. This is in contrast to scientific languages in which the relationship between meaning and its representation is isomorphic; in other words, in scientific languages a meaning is associated with a single, or sometimes several – specific - ways of representing it.

Subsequent chapters in the book will demonstrate a novel instructional and assessment methodology for deep comprehension in several content areas and sign systems, based on the rich literature on word meaning and concept formation in linguistics and semiotics on the one hand, and in developmental and cognitive psychology on the other (Juhasz, Yap, Dicke, Taylor, & Gullick, 2011), and show how independent studies in these disciplines converge on the necessary clues for constructing a procedure for the demonstration of mastery of knowledge, with equivalence-of-meaning across multiple representations. Following are brief overviews of each chapter in the book.

Chapter 1: This chapter describes a novel pedagogy for conceptual thinking and peer cooperation with Meaning Equivalence Reusable Learning Objects (MERLO) that enhance higher-order thinking; deepens comprehension of conceptual content; and improves learning outcomes. The evolution of this instructional methodology follows insights from recent research and developments in digital information; analysis of patterns of evolving concepts in human experience, that led to the emergence of concept science; research in neuroscience and brain imaging, showing that exposure of learners to multi-semiotic problems enhance cognitive control of inter-hemispheric attentional processing in the lateral brain, and increase higher-order thinking. Multi-semiotic representations of conceptual meaning are found in most knowledge domains where issues of quantity, structure, space, and change play important roles: In science (physics; biology); as well as in applied sciences - medicine, engineering; in mathematics and statistics; and in social science, where language, images, and mathematical symbolism - as well as other sign systems - are regularly used to encode meaning. To teach architecture, either by analyzing step by step design process or via exploring history of ideas manifested through built form, is to work on interpretation of precedent that conveys an idea within certain time, at a given level of technology, and with corresponding language of formal artistic expression; the specific concepts develop in a context of cultural changes, technological advancement, and evolving functional criteria. Teaching courses in History and Theory of Architecture to young architecture students with pedagogy for conceptual thinking enhance higher-order thinking, deepen comprehension of conceptual content, and improve learning outcomes; it allows to connect analysis of historic artifact, identify pattern of design ideas extracted from the precedent and transfer concepts of good design into the individual's creative design process.

Chapter 2: Effects of availability of digital knowledge on teaching, learning, and assessment, and the emergence of pedagogy for conceptual thinking with meaning equivalence in different knowledge domains in early digital era. It includes three proof-of-concept implementations of Meaning Equivalent Reusable Learning Objects (MERLO) in three different contexts: Course 'Risk management in the supply chain' at Material and Manufacturing Ontario (MMO) Centre of Excellence, in 2002, to evaluate the potential of MERLO to assess and improve learning outcomes in workplace workshops to be offered jointly by MMO and University of Toronto Innovation Foundation. In 2004, secondary school courses in mathematics, physics, and chemistry at Russian Academy of Sciences, Ioffe Physical-Technical Institute, Lycee 'Physical-Technical High School' at St. Petersburg, to train teachers in administering MERLO formative assessments and evaluate learning outcomes in STEM courses (Science, Technology, Engineering, and Mathematics). In 2006, implementing MERLO pedagogy, including development of MERLO databases for grades 9 – 12 mathematics courses at Independent Learning Center (ILC) of TVOntario. MERLO is a multi-dimensional database that allows the sorting and mapping of important concepts through multi-semiotic representations in multiple sign systems, including: target statements of particular conceptual situations, and relevant other statements. MERLO evaluates the learner's depth of understanding of newly acquired concepts and skills. Pedagogy for Conceptual Thinking include Meaning Equivalence Reusable Learning Objects (MERLO), in reusable on-line databases, each containing item-families that cover both the conceptual content as well as practical skills in a specific content.

Chapter 3: Concept Parsing Algorithms (CPA) is a novel learning tool in the context of pedagogy for conceptual thinking. It supports semantic searches of Key Word In Context (KWIC), an interactive procedure that use text analysis (concordance; collocation; co-occurrence; word frequency) and allows students to explore the course Knowledge Repository (KR) for discovery of conceptual content. InCoD guides sequential teaching/learning episodes in an academic course by focusing learners' attention on conceptual meaning. InCoD is part of a pedagogical approach that is very different from the usual classroom scenario where students are given a problem-solving exercise and asked to solve it individually. Pedagogy for conceptual thinking include weekly formative assessments, structured to provide opportunities for students to discuss and exchange ideas; to share and contrast points-of-view; to prompt and refresh each other's memory regarding important details of the conceptual situation; and to 'compare notes' about possible responses. In weekly searches with InCoD the learner reads and annotates found documents, and evaluates their degree of relevance to the specific conceptual situation under consideration; creates his/her Individual Index with alphabetic list of content words and annotations; and constructs concept maps with graphical visualizations that reveal patterns of associations among concepts. InCoD semantic searches prompt class discussions and lead to discovery of relations among co-occurring, subordinate concepts. They provide feedback that identify 'soft conceptual spots' in students' current understanding of important conceptual issues, and guide the instructor to initiate class activities to remedy conceptual misunderstandings. Systematic video recordings of small group discussions in weekly formative quizzes reveal enhanced students' engagement and peer cooperation, and members of a group listening intently to an individual presenting a convincing point-of-view. Pedagogy of conceptual thinking and peer cooperation in the classroom motivate and engage students, enhance learning outcomes and higher-order thinking. This is particularly important in large undergraduate classes.

Chapter 4: This chapter looks at an in depth application of Meaning Equivalence Reusable Learning Objects (MERLO) to mathematics education and teachers' professional development. The study has been conducted during professional development courses for in-service teachers, and is focused on mathematics teachers' praxeologies, namely their didactical techniques and theoretical aspects embraced to accomplish a task. Specifically, the task given to the teachers consists in designing MERLO items to be used in their classrooms, working in groups or individually, after having been trained by researchers in mathematical education. The chapter presents two case studies with data, one dealing with secondary school teachers in Italy and one concerning primary teachers in Australia. One of the main aims of the study is the analysis of the praxeologies of these teachers when they are engaged in designing MERLO items during professional development programs. The chapter demonstrates, with these examples, the generalizability potential of MERLO items and that they can be used in different cultural and institutional ecosystems.

What was observed in the two experiments in Italy and Australia is that, even if the teachers come from different school levels and have worked differently on MERLO items (in Italy in groups, in Australia individually) they developed quite similar praxeologies of design, based on common institutional necessities, mathematical coherence, and didactical knowledge. For example, Italian teachers worked on the design of items starting from questions taken by national assessment (INVALSI test for secondary level), and Australian teachers for building items took their inspiration by national curriculum. Particularly, similarities in the process of selecting the five statements for the item, as a technique of the praxeology were observed. The practical component can be summarized into three main steps: 1) the selection of a mathematical concept or meaning (frequencies in Italy, fractions in Australia); 2) the construction of statements sharing the same meaning with different registers of representations (numerical, graphical, verbal); and 3) the introduction of other statements that represent different concepts or meaning with respect to the previous ones (different distributions of frequencies in Italy, different values of fractions in Australia). Similarities were also documented in the theoretical counterpart of the praxeology. The two criteria of Meaning Equivalence and Surface Similarity, the mathematical and pedagogical knowledge and the institutional references appear both in Italy and in Australia as justification of the technique applied in the selection and design of the single statements. It is possible to justify these similarities with invariants involved in designing an item: the mathematical content, the same in different countries, and the MERLO framework, also the same in both groups because it is based on the same criteria (meaning equivalence and surface similarity). These observations suggest that MERLO items can be used in different countries by adapting them to institutional contexts, while retaining their substantial structure.

Chapter 5: Evidence based medicine (EMB) is the process of systematically finding, appraising, and using contemporaneous research findings as the basis for clinical decisions. It relies on a uniform, conscious process of integration of individual clinical expertise with an agreed-upon interpretation of the best available, valid systematic research about what interventions have been shown to work in specific circumstances. This chapter describes situations in which – apparently - during an informed consent, patients remember little of the information given, and their comprehension level is often overestimated by physicians. This study measures level of understanding of informed consent for elective cesarean surgery using an Evidence Based Informed Consent (EBIC) model based on six MERLO assessments. MERLO recognition and production scores and follow-up interviews of 50 patients and their partners were recorded. Statistical comparison of scores within couples was performed by weighted kappa agreement, t-tests and Ward's hierarchical clustering. Recognition score means were high for patients and partners with low standard deviation (SD), while production scores means were lower with higher SD. Clustering analysis showed that only 70% (35/50) of couples were assigned to the same cluster and t-test yields significant difference of scores within couple. Kappa yields moderate agreement levels on all items except for items in two specific topic areas which are lower. Follow-up interviews show that participants consider MERLO assessments to be helpful in improving comprehension.

Chapter 6: This chapter reviews the literature regarding Concept maps (Cmaps), that were described as a successful way to make knowledge structures visible. During a Cmap task elaboration, novice students are likely to suffer cognitive overload, and they might avoid coping with difficult contents staying in his/her semantic safe territory. The authors have developed an innovative approach using Cmaps with embedded errors applied on Sero! – a cloud-based knowledge assessment platform. This chapter presents a case study involving the current use of Cmaps with errors as an assessment task capable of identifying misconceptions about the advances of molecular biology. Undergraduate students (n=86) were asked to find the errors hidden in the propositional network. The results highlighted the importance of being aware of errors with different levels of difficulty and the possibility to categorize the types of errors added to the Cmap. The task challenged the students to go beyond their safe semantic territory. Misconceptions were readily identified from the students' answers providing good insights for the development of a bespoke feedback. The current data available is enough to foresee a broad range of research opportunities to readers interested in concept mapping, instruction and learning analytics.

REFERENCES

Ellerman. (2009). Counting distinctions: on the conceptual foundations of Shannon's information theory. *Synthese, 168*, 119–149. DOI doi:10.100711229-008-9333-7

Evans, V. (2006). Lexical concepts, cognitive models and meaning-construction. *Cognitive Linguistics, 17*(4), 491–534. doi:10.1515/COG.2006.016

Gergen, K. J. (1994). The communal creation of meaning. In W. F. Overton & D. S. Palermo (Eds.), The nature and ontogenesis of meaning. Hillsdale, NJ: Lawrence Erlbaum Associates.

Ivanov, V. V. (1976). *Ocherki po istorii semiotiki v SSSR*. Moscow: NAUK.

Ivanov, V. V. (1977). The role of semiotics in the cybernetic study of man and collective. In D. P. Lucid (Ed.), Soviet Semiotics (pp. 27–38). Baltimore, MD: John Hopkins University Press. (Original publication 1965)

Juhasz, B. J., Yap, M. J., Dicke, J., Taylor, S. C., & Gullick, M. M. (2011). Rapid communication: Tangible words are recognized faster: The grounding of meaning in sensory and perceptual systems. *Quarterly Journal of Experimental Psychology, 64*(9), 1683–1691. doi:10.1080/17470218.2011.605150 PMID:21892884

Kintsch, W., & Mangalath, P. (2011). The Construction of Meaning. *Topics in Cognitive Science, 3*, 346–370. Doi:10.1111/j.1756-8765.2010.01107.x

Shannon, C. E. (1948). A methematical theory of information. *The Bell System Technical Journal, 27*(3), 379–423, 623–656. doi:10.1002/j.1538-7305.1948.tb01338.x

Smith, L. D. (1997). Historical and philosophical foundations of the problem of meaning. In C. Mandell & A. McCabe (Eds.), *The problem of meaning: Behavioral and cognitive perspectives* (pp. 15–79). Amsterdam: Elsevier. doi:10.1016/S0166-4115(97)80133-1

Uspensky, B. A. (1977). Semiotics of art. In D. P. Lucid (Ed.), Soviet semiotics: An anthology (pp. 171–173). Baltimore, MD: John Hopkins University Press. (Original publication 1962)

Chapter 1
High Order of Conceptual Thinking:
Find the Equivalence of Meaning

Masha Etkind
Ryerson University, Canada

ABSTRACT

This chapter describe a novel pedagogy for conceptual thinking and peer cooperation with meaning equivalence reusable learning objects (MERLO) that enhances higher-order thinking; it deepens comprehension of conceptual content and improves learning outcomes. The evolution of this instructional methodology follows insights from recent developments: analysis of patterns of evolving concepts in human experience that led to the emergence of concept science, development of digital information, research in neuroscience and brain imaging showing that exposure of learners to multi-semiotic problems enhance cognitive control of inter-hemispheric attentional processing in the lateral brain, and increase higher-order thinking. The research on peer cooperation and indirect reciprocity document the motivational effect of being observed, a psychological imperative that motivates individuals to cooperate and to contribute to better common knowledge. Teaching courses in History and Theory of Architecture to young architecture students with pedagogy for conceptual thinking enhance higher-order thinking, deepen comprehension of conceptual content, and improve learning outcomes; it allows one to connect analysis of historic artifact, identify pattern of design ideas extracted from the precedent, and transfer concepts of good design into the individual's creative design process.

DOI: 10.4018/978-1-7998-1985-1.ch001

INTRODUCTION

Higher Order Of Thinking With Meaning Equivalence Reusable Learning Objects (Merlo)

'...In all matters, but particularly in architecture, there are these two points: the thing signified, and that which gives it its significance. That which is signified is the subject of which we may be speaking; and that which gives significance is a demonstration on scientific principles. It appears, then, that one who professes himself an architect should be well versed in both directions. He ought, therefore, to be both naturally gifted and amenable to instruction.'

Vitruvius (70–15 BC). 10 Books on Architecture. Book1: The education of the architect.

The main goal of this chapter is to describe innovative way of teaching and learning architecture with pedagogy for conceptual thinking that focus learners' attention on conceptual meaning of form, and enhance learning outcomes from understanding concepts extracted from architecture precedent into design. This chapter discuss the specifics of teaching architecture with Meaning Equivalence Reusable Learning Objects (MERLO), and describes pedagogy for conceptual thinking as applied in study of architecture and peer cooperation that enhance higher-order thinking, deepen comprehension of conceptual content, and enrich interactive learning processes that lead to better understanding of principles and can be then applied in the field of architecture (Shafrir & Etkind, 2018; Etkind, Kenett, & Shafrir, 2016; Shafrir & Kenett, 2016; Shafrir, Etkind, & Treviranus, 2006; Ripley, Etkind, & Shafrir, 2004).

MERLO is a multi-dimensional database that allows the sorting and mapping of important concepts through multi-semiotic representations in multiple sign systems, including: exemplary target statements of particular conceptual situations, and relevant other statements. Each node of MERLO database is an item family that includes five statements: one Target Statement (TS) that describes a conceptual situation and encodes different features of an important concept; and 4 other statements that are sorted by two sorting criteria:

- Shared equivalence-of-meaning with TS.
- Shared surface similarity with TS.

Figure 1 is a template for constructing an item family anchored in a single target statement (TS). Statements populating the four quadrants of the template in Figure 1, namely, Q1; Q2; Q3; Q4; are thematically sorted by their relation to TS. For

Figure 1. Template for constructing an item-family in MERLO

	Surface similarity [SS]		
Q1	Yes	No	Q2
SS	Yes	SS No	
ME	Yes	ME Yes	
SS	Yes	SS No	
Q3 ME	No	ME No	Q4

TARGET STATEMENT — Meaning equivalence [ME] Yes / No

MERLO: Item family

example, if a statement contains text in natural language, then by 'surface similarity' we mean same/similar words appearing in the same/similar order as in the TS; and by 'meaning equivalence' we mean that in a community that shares a sublanguage (Cabre, 1998; Kittredge, 1983) with a controlled vocabulary, a majority would likely agree that the meaning of the statement being sorted is equivalent to the meaning of TS. In Figure 1, statements in quadrants Q1 and Q3 are similar in appearance to TS, which means that they share the same sign-system with TS (e.g., text). In contrast, statements in quadrants Q2 and Q4 are not similar in appearance to TS, which means that these statements may be constructed within another sign-system (e.g., images; diagrams); or they may be constructed in the same sign system as TS, but do not look similar to TS.

The 4 quadrants contain the following types of statements:

- Q1 contains statements similar in appearance to TS and shares equivalence-of-meaning with it.
- Q2 contains statements that are not similar in appearance to TS, but do share equivalence-of-meaning with it.
- Q3 contains statements similar in appearance to TS, but that do not share equivalence-of-meaning with it.

Figure 2. Example of MERLO assessment item with Target Statement on 'Greek Acropolis'; TS; plus Q2; Q3; and Q4 statements

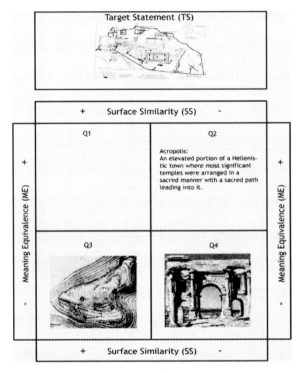

- Q4 contains statements that, although thematically relevant to TS, are not similar in appearance to TS and do not share equivalence-of-meaning with it.

Collectively, MERLO item families encode the conceptual mapping that covers the full content of a course (a particular content area within a discipline, for example 'functions' in mathematics). MERLO pedagogy guides sequential teaching/learning episodes in a course by focusing learners' attention on meaning. The format of a MERLO assessment item allows the instructor to assess deep comprehension of conceptual content by eliciting responses that signal learners' ability to recognize, and to produce, multiple representations, in multiple sign-systems - namely, multi-semiotic - that share equivalence-of-meaning. A typical MERLO assessment item contains 5 unmarked statements: unmarked TS (target statement); plus four additional (unmarked) statements from quadrants Q2; Q3; and Q4. Our experience has shown that inclusion of statements from quadrant Q1 makes a MERLO assessment item too easy, because it gives away the shared meaning due to the valence-match between surface similarity and meaning equivalence - a strong indicator of shared meaning between a Q1 and TS. Therefore, Q1 statements are excluded from MERLO assessment items.

Task instructions for MERLO assessment are:

At least two – possibly more - out of the five statements share equivalence-of meaning

- *Mark all statements – **but only those** – that share equivalence-of-meaning*
- *Formulate the shared concept*

Following these task instructions, learner's response to a MERLO item combines two formats: (i) multiple-choice/multiple-response (***recognition***); and (ii) short written answer (***production***). Subsequently, there are two scores for each MERLO item: recognition score; and production score.

Figure 3 is an example of a MERLO item in 2nd year course 'History of Architecture', that includes 5 representations (at least two of which share equivalence-of-meaning), in the following sign-systems: urban plan (A); photograph (B); orthogonal drawing (C); language (D); 3D sketch (E).

Figure 3. Example of a multi-semiotic MERLO item (History of Architecture, Italian Baroque)

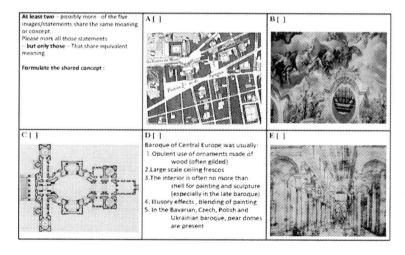

Learning From Precedent: Analytical Interpretation

'...cornerstone of effective learning, understanding facts and ideas in the context of a conceptual framework as ways of thinking that explore patterns of equivalence-of-meaning in ideas, relations, and underlying issues.'

Bransford, Brown & Cocking (2004).

In teaching and addressing issues in a discipline that operates within visual and contextual content, one relies on interpretation of form and its conceptual meaning. The increasing interest in architectural history and attention to historic precedent has focused on the relationship between history and design. History studied in the academic sense of seeing a place within a continuum, or in the strictly scholarly sense of knowing the past, can limit our knowledge of architecture to little more than names, dates, and style recognition. It is the ability to recognize concepts that share equivalence of meaning within or beyond of historical context that helps architects recognise and understand the true meaning of form.

To recognize guiding principles of good design one must understand architectural precedent and should be able to decompose the main design idea of the precedent into numerous sets of meaningful concepts. How does one recognize the conceptual meaning of form - the elements of totality of formal expression, the distinction of the composition of parts from a whole, of the material construct, of the tangible function and intangible narrative, of the path through time and space? Pedagogy based on recognition of Meaning Equivalence is a helpful tool that may lead the way. Pedagogy for conceptual thinking focuses learners' attention on meaning and enhances their understanding of the difference between formal representations that 'look alike' but do not share the equivalence-of-meaning and those examples that share same essential characteristics without apparent similarity. To recognize meaning in architecture one needs to search for evocative concepts that constitute comprehensive architectural statement. While the final outcome of architecture is the one that constitutes physical reality of built form, a material construct that integrates ideas of the time, and represents level of available technology - the interpretation of form that conveys meaningful relations associated with place and time is an intellectual task of decoding the abstract ideas and clarifying intangible connections between the concepts.

Simple recognition of architectural idea in a precedent of good design - even though may serve on its own as a design tool - does not yet necessarily lead to the good design outcome. An ability to recognize meaningful connections between good designs concepts make a designer aware of a pattern attributed to good design. While not lessening the importance of concern for other issues guiding design and for the design process, recognition of meaning equivalence between dissimilar representations of a concept establishes higher level of conceptual appreciation of a good design pattern. Recognition of commonality of a concept present in a good building from one period in history with those of other times demonstrates one understands basic architectural ideas which are recognizable as formative patterns. To introduce Meaning Equivalence Methodology into teaching architecture is to establish a measure and criteria for understanding of architectural history; by examining basic similarities of good designs over time, by identifying generic solutions to design problems which transcend time, and by developing a conceptual instrument for analysis of form, one develops a tool that ultimately guides good design.

Equivalence of Meaning in Architecture

'These spontaneously formulated statements of complex issues are often encoded in alternative representations in different sign systems (e.g., text; images; diagrams; equations) that illustrate different aspects of the conceptual situation under discussion. It is the meaning that is important, not the sign. We can change the sign, but retain the meaning.' Vygotsky (1930/1984; p. 74).

Multi-semiotic representations of conceptual meaning are found in most knowledge domains where issues of quantity, structure, space, and change play important roles: In science (physics; biology); as well as in applied sciences - medicine, engineering; in mathematics and statistics; and in social science, where language, images, and mathematical symbolism - as well as other sign systems - are regularly used to encode meaning. To teach architecture, either by analyzing step by step design process or via exploring history of ideas manifested through built form, is to work on interpretation of precedent that conveys an idea within certain time, at a given level of technology, and with corresponding language of formal artistic expression; the specific concepts develop in a context of cultural changes, technological advancement, and evolving functional criteria. (Radford, Srivastava & Morkoc, 2014).

MERLO pedagogy guides sequential teaching/learning episodes in a course by focusing learners' attention on meaning. The format of a MERLO assessment item allows the instructor to assess deep comprehension of conceptual content by eliciting responses that signal learners' ability to recognize, and to produce, multiple representations, in multiple sign-systems - namely, multi-semiotic - that share equivalence-of-meaning. In a classroom that include regular discussions of Meaning Equivalence in architectural history, as well as weekly practice of MERLO for formative assessments - and in assessing midterm and final exams - MERLO develops into an effective vehicle for discussions focused on architectural ideas through the use of precedent in time. The understanding of architectural history derives from profound conceptual investigation that develops knowledge and understanding focused on recognition of meaningful ideas, not just on names and dates. MERLO allows the instructor to identify an actual level of each individual student's comprehension of architectural concept, based on his/her own understanding of development of ideas through history and on the ability to follow the evolution of architectural form through time. The noticeable compensation for extra effort invested into deeper conceptual formal analysis with use of MERLO provides a student-designer with vocabulary that, while developed individually, has been tested through history of architectural practice. Young designers benefit from a comprehensive understanding of formative ideas, as well as organizational, material, aesthetical, structural and other concepts influencing the design. (Clark & Pause, 2012; Borden & Andrews, 2014).

An ability to transfer conceptual understanding of meaning equivalence across dissimilar sign systems in multi-semiotic contexts is of particular importance for architects. Any architectural project incorporates multiple criteria and integrates diverse measures of both qualitative and quantitative responses to a given task. Multiple representations of a given concept address the same issues from different directions; it helps formulate variety of responses to diverse aspects of the task. And since architectural response to verbally formulated task is graphical and visual in its language, quantitative in its limitations, material in its final realisation, the multi-semiotic representation of every aspect of project is essential for the field of architecture and design. Meanwhile, the assessment of conceptual thinking of a designer, as well as that of the conceptual interpretation of the design task, typically includes unstructured items, questions that focus on the meaning of conceptual situations: '...this sets the mind free to do what it does best - be inductively creative' (Box, 1997, p. 49).

In architectural precedent one looks for dissimilar representations or various ideas and concepts extracted from a given example while recognising the existence of parts of a bigger whole; one recognizes the conceptual 'DNA' of a design concept of the precedent. Meaning Equivalence, as a construct, indicates commonality of conceptual meaning across different representations of ideas within and across sign systems. 'The related construct of representational competence is the ability to recognize and to trans-code equivalence-of-meaning in multiple, multi-semiotic representations within and across sign systems (Sigel, 1954; 1993; 1999), and to re-represent equivalent meaning by incorporating higher-order relations within and/ or across different sign systems (Shafrir, 1999).

Meaning Equivalence methodology as used in analysing formative concepts in architectural precedent becomes a useful tool for understanding and assessing architectural work of the past and for creating new architecture; it provides a device for connecting meaningful architectural ideas regardless of their origin and time. Thus, it provides the opportunity to transcend culture, period, and what we call style.

It is critically important to establish that Meaning Equivalence methodology allows recognition of important concepts in design across different types of representation; it reminds us that there is more to architecture than a picture, a diagram or a well composed photograph.

Alternative Conceptual Thinkers: Thinking Outside the box, Recognizing Conceptual Sub-Set

In the context of a given lecture, and during a follow-up discussion focused on the meaning of introduced concepts, at some point of discourse one can expect the class to follow certain logic determined by the intellectual interpretation of relationship and equivalency of conceptual meaning presented by the lecturer. Therefore, the instructor can expect certain common interpretation of architectural idea and its implication in the context of presented material. One anticipates and regularly receives an expected logical outcome, a predicted formulation of conceptual meaning based on the contextual logic of the given discussion. One, though, cannot always take that outcome for granted. More so, one should expect multiple interpretations of possible equivalence-of-meanings from a creative group. And while the majority of the class will follow the expected path of discussion, the more independent minds will take some alternative paths.

Focusing on Meaning Equivalence allows weekly class discussions that clarify concepts introduced during the lecture (see: Arzarello, Kenett, Robutti, Shafrir, Prodromou & Carante, 2015). In order to prepare weekly quizzes that follow the lectures, the instructor composes a MERLO item that addresses at least one of multiple topics covered in the lecture. One of the main concepts of the lecture usually is selected as a target statement; and Q2, Q3 and Q4 are usually formulating expected outcomes of the logic of the discussion. But there may be curious nonconformities. For example, while giving a lecture on architecture and planning in classical Greece, a number of topics are being discussed, such as: application and semiotics of classical order; relationship between elements in planning of the temple; materiality and planning of typical residential building; and - among many other topics - the planning concept of the masterplan of Greek Acropolis. In discussing the planning principles of Greek Acropolis one expects recognition of several converging aspects of the planning idea. By recognizing in the Acropolis the organizational principle of geometry of golden proportion in the position of temples on the elevated plateau of the hill; by identifying the processional entrance into the urban space of the Acropolis via a monumental path leading up to the Acropolis through a gateway, a prototypical Greek propylaea that serves as the entrance to the Acropolis in Athens; or by identifying the relationship between the Acropolis and the agora; one recognizes the planning concept of Acropolis.

Figure 4 is an example of MERLO quiz where the shared concept of Propylaea, as a processional and monumental entrance into Acropolis acted as a symbolic partition between the secular and religious parts of a city. The 5 options in this MERLO were:

(A) = orthogonal plan of Minoan Knossos Palace is Q3.
(B) = T (Target Statement), orthogonal plan of Acropolis Propylaea.
(C) = 3D view of Propylaea leading into Acropolis in Athens is Q2.
(D) = verbal definition of Propylaea as a 'monumental gate or entranceway to a specific space, usually to a temple or religious complex and as such a symbolic partition between the secular and religious parts of a city' is another Q2.
(E) = image of Roman Triumphal Arch of Constantine is Q4.

The correct answer expected for this MERLO was to be selected (V = YES) are options (B), C), and (D) as statements sharing the equivalent meaning; option (A) and was correctly not to be selected (X = NO); option (E) was not to be selected, but incorrectly selected.

This MERLO assessment was given to class of 100 students as a MERLO quiz in the course 'Ideas, Technologies and Precedents I' after a lecture that discussed urban planning principles of Greek city; the concept of secular vs. religious separation of *Ancient Greek town* was one of the key concepts discussed in the lecture. In this MERLO quiz students were expected to recognize the Propylaea of the Greek Acropolis and to identify it as an entrance into sacred Acropolis as a concept of

Figure 4. Thinking out of the box

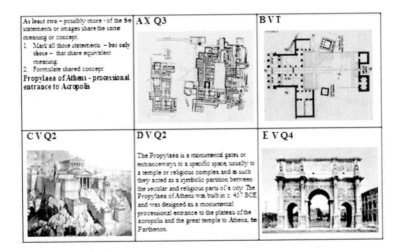

Greek town planning. It was also meant for students to recognize that an arch was not part of Ancient Greek civilization, and therefore, not to be included into the set of selected items that shared the equivalence of meaning.

While majority of the class followed the expected path of thought, few students identified a different concept in the MERLO; the alternative shared equivalence of meaning was that of a general concept of "processional way". These students (three out of 100) defined a "Processional Path in Ancient city" as shared equivalence of meaning between the Greek Propylaea and the Roman Arch. The selected choice for the alternative concept was (B), (C), and (E). For an instructor marking the quiz and looking for correct answers it is critical to identify these students who are thinking out of the box and to make sure that their alternative way of thinking is recognized. In many cases these are most creative and most innovative conceptual thinkers in the group.

Concept Mapping: The Context

Meaning Equivalence pedagogy for conceptual thinking incorporates a model of concept mapping as a way to develop logical thinking and enhance study skills by revealing connections and helping students to see how individual ideas form a larger whole. Concept map in essence is a description of the organization of meaningful concepts in a context of the discipline that are related to each other. Proximity of those conceptual statements indicates similarity in meaning, though there is a border beyond which the shared meaning is gone. Concept maps enhance metacognition (learning to learn, and thinking about knowledge); improve semantic ability; assess student's understanding of learning objectives, concepts, and the relationship among those concepts. Meaning Equivalence, on the other hand, is a construct that - in addition – also signifies commonality of meaning across representations: a polymorphous - one-to-many - transformation of meaning. By recognizing the meaning equivalence through dissimilarity of formal appearances of its parts, one identifies the totality of meaning: a delineated area on concept map that shows conceptual commonality. It is by placing conceptual statements that in essence transmit similar meaning in architecture into a context of their time and function that allows us to define conceptual similarities and attribute deeper meaning to understanding of their differences. By thinking beyond the context introduced at the lecture that was recognized by majority of students in the class as shared meaning, somebody in the class was thinking differently, unconventionally, recognizing different aspects of the concept. Post quiz class discussion allowed the whole class to hear a new argument, and to recognize meaning equivalence from a different perspective. Thinking outside the box by one person in a group elevates the class discussion and demonstrates different level of conceptual thinking. It is critically important to demonstrate to the group the ability of a student to think differently, unconventionally; to recognize his/her diverse ability to see the unforeseen aspects of otherwise logically framed concept, ability to recognize other than expected context for a shared concept in a given MERLO.

MERLO: Building Blocks in Study of Architecture

How to construct a MERLO for the study of architecture that will enhance clarity of thinking and advance design skills? What are the items that should constitute MERLO in the field of architecture? By decomposing and therefore separating individual concepts from a comprehensive expression and by identifying their partial meaningful roles in 'part to a whole' relationship, one begins to understand a picture of total meaning in architecture as its essence. To offer students of architecture a set of architectural ideas, where they have to identify the equivalence of meaning, one allows students to clarify ideas and to show a level conceptual comprehension of the topic discussed. By recognizing equivalence of meaning among dissimilar representations of a shared conceptual meaning, a student demonstrates good understanding of the topic. The contextual interpretation of the set in some cases may offer different interpretation of the equivalency of meaning. While composing MERLO for a discourse on meaning in architectural concepts, one is becoming acutely aware of the significance of context for the performed analysis. The definition of relationship of 'part to a whole' depends on the anticipated interpretation of a whole.

Renaissance is one striking example in history when ideas and concepts from different areas of knowledge and art overlapped and impacted on each other. It is obvious that during that period of powerful universal totality of ideas by looking at the components and recognizing the attributes of a whole, one recognizes meaning equivalence encoded in different representations and different aspects of big concept of human being in the center of the universe. The idea of a Vitruvian man as a centre of the Renaissance universe, and Philippe Brunelleschi's invention of one point perspective that provides viewer with a perception of anticipated 3D space, as well as the idea of 'domed centralized space', all these ideas - while influencing one another - recognize concept of space that emphasizes the significance of man's place in the universe. One becomes aware of the paradigm shift from the world of Middle Age with its religious focus on spirituality of light and verticality leading into heaven, to the Renaissance universe focused on intellectual power of man. This change of conceptual idea of the time cannot be understood through decomposition of isolated architectural precedents but should be presented and comprehended in a context of - and through a sub-set of concepts - converging into a bigger idea of Renaissance universe. The MERLO for that bigger idea would expect learners to find the intersection of ideas where they all converge into a bigger concept of

Renaissance. It will require learners to exercise a significantly higher level of conceptual comprehension to recognize meaning equivalence shared not only across different forms of representation, but across different areas and forms of knowledge.

Fig 5 shows MERLO where various ideas applied in architecture of Renaissance period converge into one inclusive idea. Four out of five design ideas converge into one comprehensive concept of the Italian Renaissance. The items in this MERLO display the following:

(A) = One point perspective representation of space as perceived by an observer (man in the space) - Q2.

    B = T is the concept of a 'Man as a Center of Universe'.
    C = Q2 – proportions as a basic principle for harmony in design composition.
    D = Q3 – regulating lines in work of Le Corbusier.
    E = Q2 – centralized space of a Renaissance Church covered with a large dome, in this case the Duomo by Brunelleschi.

In solving this MERLO, students are expected to recognize the fact that Le Corbusier's facades, while demonstrating visually similar approach to composition by using the regulating lines, do not belong to the same set of sub-concepts that form

Figure 5. MERLO based on the intersection of ideas (sub-concepts)

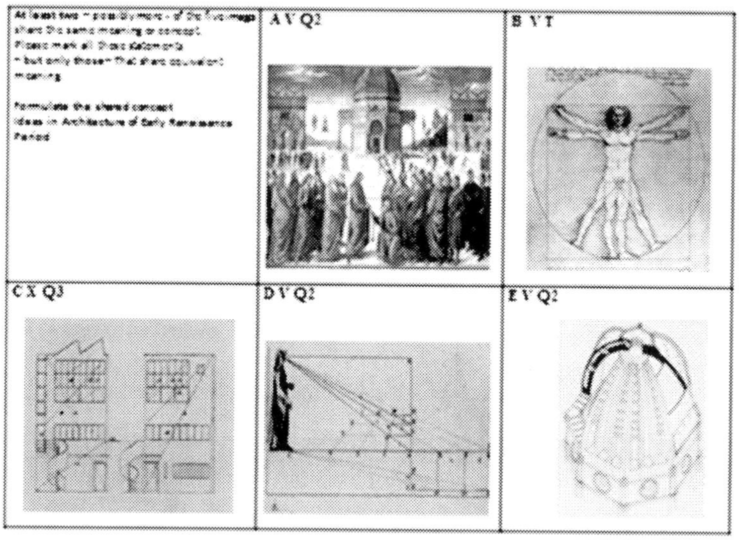

a comprehensive idea of the Renaissance. As periods in history come closer to our time, the ideas extracted from the examined precedents become more relevant to architects as design tools. The design concepts of modernity are discussed in class, and as discussion progresses the more complex level of equivalence of meaning is addressed and is reflected in the composition of MERLO. While looking at the work of modern masters, students are expected to recognize contemporary ideas and principles of design at more multidimensional and complex levels of the equivalency of meaning. Surface similarity may often be confused with similar meaning in the world of technology defining aesthetics of form. For example, in a MERLO composed to demonstrate Le Corbusier's use of proportions and regulating lines - an insightful understanding that le Corbusier developed while studying classical and traditional architecture - one should be clearly aware of history of architecture. The language of modern architecture is not explicit in defining recognizable iconographic form. Representation of form stripped of decorating ornamentation and expression of finishing materials leaves an uninformed viewer confused in an attempt to find informing precedent. It is through relationship across time between precedents of good design that one gets to understand ideas of the modern time. In analysing the precedent to Le Corbusier's La Tourette, one should be able to recognize a fundamental principle of design based on the relationship between Fibonacci Numbers Theory to anthropometric scale of proportions described by Le Corbusier in the Modulor. By comparing the role of Golden Ratio in forming proportions in classical Greek design to le Corbusier's ideas of the Modulor, one recognizes the concepts of shared conceptual meaning traced as elements of good design across time (Clark & Pause, 2012).

To solve the MERLO in Fig 6, what are the images to be selected as shared equivalence of meaning if to assume that the shared meaning is 'Use of Proportions in Design'? MERLO items (A), (B), (C), and (D) are to be selected to identify use of proportions in design. Some students may superficially identify the shared meaning by simply recognizing the work of Le Corbusier. The task expects good learners to recognize and interpret the ideas commonly shared by certain projects and not by other ones. The deeper the student's understanding of contextual proximity of common ideas, the narrower becomes the equivalency of conceptual meaning and the proximity of TS to Q2. The Q3, on the other hand, can turn into Q2 as the context of identified shared meaning shifts.

The deeper thinking student understands the contextual proximity of common ideas in design, the more precise gets the definition of equivalency of shared meaning, and greater is the proximity of TS and Q2 on the conceptual map. Ability to identify the closer related concepts and by recognizing the meaning equivalency

Figure 6. MERLO: Equivalence of meaning recognized across time: use of proportions in design

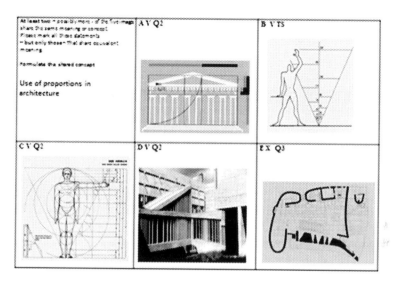

through dissimilarity of closer ideas through the elements of the formal appearance of its parts, one identifies greater totality as summary of meaning. It is by placing conceptual statements that in essence transmit similar meaning, into a context of their time and their function, that allows us to define similarities and attribute deeper meaning to understanding their differences. By asking students to identify the meaning equivalence between totally dissimilar representations or - on the other hand - to recognize the different meaning behind the misleadingly close surface similarities, one clarifies the depth of understanding of otherwise an opaque and complex conceptual representation in architecture.

Good vs. Poor Conceptual Thinkers

Following numerous evaluative implementations of MERLO pedagogy (Etkind, Kenett, & Shafrir, 2010; Shafrir & Etkind, 2006), we defined **good conceptual thinkers** as those students who score **high** *on both recognition and production on MERLO items;* and **poor conceptual thinkers** *as those students who score* **low** *on both recognition and production on MERLO items.*

In order to clearly identify good vs. poor conceptual thinkers, we operationalized the above definition as follows: We convert MERLO raw scores for recognition and for production to Z-scores (standard scores with mean = 0.0, and standard deviation = 1.0), and define good and poor conceptual thinkers by performing a double median split of their MERLO recognition and production Z-scores in an exam in a core course in their discipline of study (i.e., course 'History of architecture' in the discipline of Architecture), as follows:

- *Good conceptual thinkers* are those who score high (above the median) on MERLO items in *recognition* of different representations that share equivalence-of-meaning; *as well as in production* of a brief written description of the concept (or idea), in the learner's mind, that led the learner to make those recognition decisions.
- In contrast, *poor conceptual thinkers* are those students who score low (at or below the median) on **both recognition and production**.

Fig. 7 is a diagrammatic representation of these definitions. As can be seen, *good conceptual thinkers* occupy the upper left part of the major diagonal, and *poor conceptual thinkers* occupy the lower right part of the major diagonal.

In an early study (Shafrir & Etkind, 2006) we investigated the question: Did 'good conceptual thinkers' also receive high scores in other courses, and did 'poor conceptual thinkers' also receive low scores in other courses? We computed Z-scores for 132 students on MERLO recognition and production scores in final exam in

Figure 7. Good vs. Poor conceptual thinkers.

	RECOGNTION Z-SCORE ABOVE	RECOGNTION Z-SCORE AT OR BELOW	
	RECOGNITON HIGH PRODUCTION HIGH GOOD CONCEPTUAL THINKERS	RECOGNITON LOW PRODUCTION HIGH	PRODUCTION Z-SCORE ABOVE
	RECOGNITON HIGH PRODUCTION LOW	RECOGNITON LOW PRODUCTION LOW POOR CONCEPTUAL THINKERS	PRODUCTION Z-SCORE AT OR BELOW

course 'History of Architecture I' taught in first year architecture; double-median split on Z-scores showed that there were 49 'good conceptual thinkers' who scored above the median (Z=0.0) on both recognition and production; and 44 were 'poor conceptual thinkers' who scored below the median on both recognition and production (in addition, there were two mixed groups). Marks of all students in the other 5 courses, plus mark on an essay in the final exam, were converted to Z-scores and are shown in Figure 8; as can be seen, *there are consistent differences between good vs. poor conceptual thinkers* in all 5 courses plus History Essay; these differences are significant at $p <= 0.01$. These results show that *MERLO pedagogy allows to distinguish good vs. poor conceptual thinkers, and to verify enhanced conceptual thinking across the curriculum.*

Is Conceptual Thinking Learnable?

One of the hypotheses tested in a recent study was that enhancing cognitive control of attentional processing of multi-semiotic MERLO items is learnable. In this study, in first year architecture course '*ASC 206: Ideas, technology, and precedents I*', 30 out of a total of 140 students registered for the course were classified in the final exam in May of 2009 as 'poor conceptual thinkers'; 25 out of these 30 students participated in a subsequent 2nd year course '*ASC 306: Ideas, technology, and*

Figure 8. Good vs. poor conceptual thinkers' z-scores in other courses

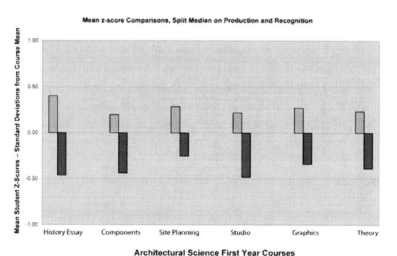

precedents II. Analysis of the Z-scores on recognition and production of each of these 25 students in the final exam of this course in December of 2009, revealed that: *14 of them improved significantly their Z-scores on recognition and/or production\; and 4 of this 14 students were elevated from the category of 'poor conceptual thinkers' in May, 2009, to the category of 'good conceptual thinkers' (high on both recognition and production) in December, 2009.*

Alternative Conceptual Thinkers

In another recent study (Etkind, Kenett & Shafrir, 2010), we tested the hypothesis that, following weekly exposure to multi-semiotic MERLO quizzes in large classes, some students develop ways of 'thinking out-of-the-box', and formulate alternative conceptual descriptions of meaning equivalence shared among representations in a MERLO assessment item. The final exam of the second year architecture course *'ASC 306: Ideas, technology, and precedents II'* in May 2011, was written by 90 students, and included 3 parts: Ten multi-semiotic MERLO assessment items; ten multiple-choice items; and an essay. Double-median-split of the Z-scores on recognition vs. production of the MERLO ítems revealed:

- 30 Good conceptual thinkers (high recognition and high production)
- 32 Poor conceptual thinkers (low recognition and low production)

In addition, ten of the 90 students were noted as having formulated *alternative descriptions of the equivalence-of-meaning* of at least one of the MERLO items; these alternative descriptions highlighted conceptual aspects that were correct, but not within the expected and obvious context of these assessment items. This study show that good conceptual thinkers scored significantly higher than poor conceptual thinkers on the essay question in the final exam; and *alternative conceptual thinkers scored significantly higher than even good conceptual thinkers did on MERLO production scores, as well as on the essay question.*

DISCUSSION

In architectural precedent one looks for dissimilar representations or various ideas and concepts extracted from a given example while recognising the existence of parts of a bigger whole; one recognizes the conceptual 'DNA' of a design concept of the precedent. Meaning Equivalence, as a construct, indicates commonality of conceptual meaning across different representations of ideas within and across sign systems. By teaching architecture with Pedagogy of Conceptual Thinking with Meaning Equivalence Reusable Learning Objects (MERLO), one works with a methodology that allows recognition of formative design ideas through various representations, and therefore identify similarity of meaning - rather than surface similarity. Recognition of Meaning Equivalence continue to be a useful means for providing a vocabulary for understanding the architectural work of others and for engaging in creating architecture. It provides a tool for connecting architectural works regardless of time or origin. Meaning Equivalence methodology, when used as pedagogy for conceptual thinking, helps instructor to guide a young architect in developing his or her own design skills; the impact of Meaning Equivalence analysis on the design process (synthesis) is clear and strong. When applied in teaching of ideas and precedents in architecture it becomes a tool for evaluation of students' level of conceptual comprehension.

When Architecture is taught with pedagogy for conceptual thinking, students develop an ability to identify patterns or connections between seemingly unrelated objects. Critical conceptual thinking is a way to enhance creativity, recognized as Higher Order Thinking Skills. Pedagogy for conceptual thinking enhances higher order thinking skills and learning outcomes, an important measure in higher education. Enhanced learning outcomes become particularly apparent in technology-enabled weekly MERLO interactive formative quizzes in large undergraduate classes. Meaning Equivalence, in essence, is a way to look behind the mirror, to peel the layers of a developed concept: a tool for deeper understanding the meaning of knowledge.

REFERENCES

Arzarello, F., Kenett, R. S., Robutti, O., Shafrir, U., Prodromou, T., & Carante, P. (2015). Teaching and assessing with new methodological tools (MERLO): A new pedagogy? *Proceedings for IMA International Conference on Barriers and Enablers to Learning Maths: Enhancing Learning and Teaching for All Learners.*

Borden, G. P., & Andrews, B. D. (2014). *Architecture Principia*. Pearson.

Box, G. (1997). Scientific Method: The Generation of Knowledge and Quality. *Quality Progress*, 47-50.

Bransford, J. D., Brown, A. L., & Cocking, R. R. (2004). *How People Learn: Brain, Mind, Experience, and School (expanded edition)*. Washington, DC: National Academy Press.

Cabre, M. T. (1998). *Terminology: Theory, Methods, and Applications*. Amsterdam: Johns Benjamins Publishing.

Clark, R. H., & Pause, M. (2012). *Precedents in Architecture: Analytic Diagrams, Formative Ideas, and Partis.* Wiley.

Etkind, M., Kenett, R. S., & Shafrir, U. (2010). The evidence-based management of learning: Diagnosis and development of conceptual thinking with meaning equivalence reusable learning objects (MERLO). Invited paper. *Proceedings of the 8th International Conference on Teaching Statistics (ICOTS8).*

Etkind, M., Kenett, R. S., & Shafrir, U. (2016). Learning in the Digital Age with Meaning Equivalence Reusable Learning Objects (MERLO). In Handbook of Research on Applied Learning Theory and Design in Modern Education, (pp. 310-333). IGI Global.

Kittredge, R. I. (1983). Sematic Processing of Texts in Restricted Sublanguages. In N. J. Cercone (Ed.), *Computational Linguistics* (pp. 45–58). Academic Press. doi:10.1016/B978-0-08-030253-9.50009-3

Radford, A., Srivastava, A., & Morkoc, S. B. (2014). *The Elements of Modern Architecture: Understanding Contemporary Buildings.* Thames and Hudson.

Ripley, C., Etkind, M., & Shafrir, U. (2004). *Teaching for Deep Comprehension with Meaning Equivalence Reusable Learning Objects: MERLO Designer's Handbook. International Society for Exploring Teaching and Learning (ISETL) Conference.* Toronto: Ryerson University.

Shafrir, U. (1999). Representational competence. In I. E. Sigel (Ed.), The Development of mental representation: Theory and applications, (pp. 371-389). Mahwah, NJ: Lawrence Erlbaum Publishers.

Shafrir, U., & Etkind, M. (2006). eLearning for Depth in the Semantic Web. *British Journal of Educational Technology, 37*(3), 425–444. doi:10.1111/j.1467-8535.2006.00614.x

Shafrir, U., & Etkind, M. (2018). Concept Parsing Algorithms (CPA) for Textual Analysis and Discovery. *Emerging Research and Opportunities.* doi:10.4018/978-1-5225-2176-1

Shafrir, U., Etkind, M., & Treviranus, J. (2006). eLearning Tools for ePortfolios. In Handbook of Research on ePortfolios (pp. 206-216). Hershey, PA: Idea Group.

Shafrir, U., & Kenett, R. S. (2016). Concept Science Evidence Based MERLO Learning Analytics. In Handbook of Research on Applied Learning Theory and Design in Modern Education, (pp. 334-357). IGI Global. doi:10.4018/978-1-4666-9634-1.ch016

Sigel, I. E. (1954). The dominance of meaning. *The Journal of Genetic Psychology, 85*(2), 201–207. doi:10.1080/00221325.1954.1053287

Sigel, I. E. (1993). The centrality of a distancing model for the development of representational competence. In R. R. Cocking & K. A. Renninger (Eds.), *The development and meaning of psychological distance* (pp. 141–158). Academic Press.

Sigel, I. E. (1999). Approaches to representation as a psychological construct: a treatise in diversity. In I. E. Sigel (Ed.), *Development of mental representation* (pp. 3–12). Lawrence Erlbaum Associates, Inc.

Vitruvius. (2014). Ten Books on Architecture (F. Granger, Trans.). Cambridge University Press.

Vygotsky, L. S. (1984). Orudie i znak v razvitii rebĕnka (Tool and sign in the development of the child). In L. S. Vygodsky (Ed.), *Sobranye Socinenij* (Vol. 6, pp. 6–90). Academic Press. (Original work published 1930)

Chapter 2

Meaning Equivalence Reusable Learning Objects (MERLO) Access to Knowledge in Early Digital Era and Development of Pedagogy for Conceptual Thinking

Uri Shafrir
University of Toronto, Canada

ABSTRACT

This chapter describes the effects of availability of digital knowledge on teaching, learning, and assessment, and the emergence of pedagogy for conceptual thinking with meaning equivalence in different knowledge domains in early digital era. It includes three proof-of-concept implementations of meaning equivalent reusable learning objects (MERLO) in three different contexts: 1) Course 'Risk management in the Supply Chain' at Material and Manufacturing Ontario (MMO) Centre of Excellence, in 2002, to evaluate the potential of MERLO to assess and improve learning outcomes in workplace workshops to be offered jointly by MMO and University of Toronto Innovation Foundation; 2) in 2004, secondary school courses in mathematics, physics, and chemistry at Russian Academy of Sciences, Ioffe Physical-Technical Institute, Lycee 'Physical-Technical High School' at St. Petersburg, to train teachers in administering MERLO formative assessments and evaluate learning outcomes in STEM courses (science, technology, engineering, and mathematics); 3) in 2006, implementing MERLO pedagogy, including development of MERLO databases for grades 9 – 12 mathematics courses at Independent Learning Center (ILC) of TVOntario.

DOI: 10.4018/978-1-7998-1985-1.ch002

INTRODUCTION

In the early 2000s 'Certificate in Conceptual Curation' was offered at iSchool Institute, Faculty of Information at University of Toronto. It provided details of important aspects of the emerging reality of digital full-text journals, books, documents, and other digitized artifacts; and the evolution of a systematic approach to the analysis of conceptual content for research, teaching and learning. The certificate was designed for teachers and librarians in secondary and post-secondary institutions, and in public and private organizations with professional learning programs, libraries and archives. It facilitated the development of innovative digital library tools that support higher-order thinking in scholarship, teaching and learning (Stafford, 2010).

Conceptual curation is a recent development in curation of large repositories containing digital full-text documents. It includes the use of semantic searches that reveal structured, multi-layered building blocks of concepts with lateral and hierarchical interactions. *Concepts* are lexically labeled patterns in the data that encode 'meaning' in different domains of knowledge: semantic content embedded in them by the situation being documented, and the specific constraints associated with data generated during this evolutionary process. The emergent discipline of *concept science* is a novel generic methodology for parsing and analyzing concepts, applicable to the various knowledge domains and professions; with tools designed for recognizing, representing, organizing, exploring, communicating, and manipulating knowledge encoded in controlled vocabularies of sublanguages (Cabre, 1998; Kittredge, 1983). Concept science documents the evolution of content and structure of concepts, and categorization, knowledge representation and use.

The rapid increase in the scope and details of information available via the Internet makes locating educational resources challenging for teachers and learners. The emerging reality of large libraries with digital, full-text documents (as well as other digital artifacts, i.e., photos, databases, diagrams, etc.) makes the development of conceptual curation - namely, a systematic approach to the analysis of concepts across large collections of digital documents - an urgent necessity (Friedman & Deek, 2003; Puntambekar & Goldstein, 2007; Neumann et al., 2017). While both digital documents, as well as traditional paper books, fall under the definition of 'artifact': *'an object that has been intentionally made or produced for a certain purpose'* (Stanford Encyclopedia of Philosophy: http://plato.stanford.edu/entries/artifact/), the universal availability and accessibility - independent on time and space - of digital artifacts, opens new horizons for research, and development of new applications. National Science Digital Library (NSDL; https://nsdl.oercommons.

org/_) was established by the National Science Foundation in 2000 as an online library with educational resources (see also: https://www.oercommons.org/) in science, technology, engineering, and mathematics (STEM). It provides access to content, services and tools that facilitate and enhance the use of this content in a variety of contexts. These sites are designed primarily for educators, but anyone can access and search the libraries at no cost. The remaining sections of this chapter will survey, discuss, and demonstrate the potential of conceptual curation to change - and enhance - the nature of scholarship, teaching and learning.

MEANING EQUIVALENCE REUSABLE LEARNING OBJECTS (MERLO)

MERLO is a multi-dimensional database that allows the sorting and mapping of important concepts through multi-semiotic representations in multiple sign systems, including: target statements of particular conceptual situations, and relevant other statements.

Each node of MERLO database (Figure 1) is an item family that includes one Target Statement (TS) that describes a conceptual situation and encodes different features of an important concept, and several other statements that populate the four

Figure 1. Template for constructing MERLO item-family

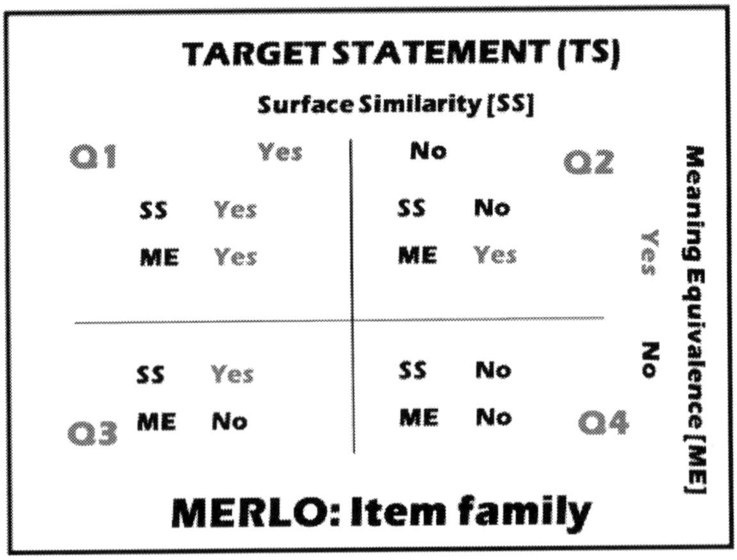

quadrants of the template in Figure 1, namely, Q1; Q2; Q3; Q4; and are thematically sorted by their relation to TS, and are organized by the following two sorting criteria:

- Shared surface similarity with TS (horizontal axis)
- Shared equivalence-of-meaning with TS (vertical axis)

For example, if a statement contains text in natural language, then by 'surface similarity' we mean same/similar words appearing in the same/similar order as in the TS; and by 'meaning equivalence' we mean that, in a community that shares a sublanguage with a controlled vocabulary (e.g., statistics; biology), a majority would likely agree that the meaning of the statement being sorted is equivalent to the meaning of TS.

In Figure 1, statements in quadrants Q1 and Q3 are similar in appearance to TS, which means that they share the same sign-system with TS (e.g., text). In contrast, statements in quadrants Q2 and Q4 are not similar in appearance to TS, which means that these statements may be constructed within another sign-system (e.g., images; symbolism); or they may be constructed by the same sign system as TS, but do not look similar to TS. Further analysis reveals that:

- Statements in quadrant *Q1* are *similar in appearance* to TS, and *share equivalence-of-meaning* with it.
- Statements in quadrant *Q3* are *similar in appearance* to TS, but *do not share equivalence-of-meaning* with it.
- Statements in quadrant *Q2* are *not similar in appearance* to TS, but *do share equivalence-of-meaning* with it.
- Finally, statements in quadrant *Q4*, although thematically relevant to TS, are *not similar in appearance* to TS and *do not share equivalence-of-meaning* with it.

Collectively, a comprehensive collection of such item families may encode the conceptual mapping that covers the full content of a course. Figure 1 is a template for constructing an item family anchored in a single target statement. The main feature of *MERLO pedagogy* is that it guides sequential teaching/learning episodes in a course by *focusing learners' attention on meaning*. The format of a MERLO assessment item allows the instructor to assess deep comprehension of conceptual content by eliciting responses that signal learners' ability to recognize, and to produce, multiple representations, in multiple sign-systems - namely, multi-semiotic - that share equivalence-of-meaning (Di Giacomo et al., 2017).

A typical MERLO assessment item contains 5 unmarked statements: unmarked TS (Target Statement) plus four additional (unmarked) statements from quadrants

Q1; Q2; Q3; and Q4. Our experience - following the MMO project described in this chapter - has shown that *inclusion of statements from quadrant Q1 makes a MERLO item too easy*, because it gives away the shared meaning due to the valence-match between surface similarity and meaning equivalence - a strong indicator of shared meaning between a Q1 and TS. However, MERLO assessment items in the early MMO project reported here *still did contain statements from quadrant Q1*.

MERLO assess the level of deep comprehension by evaluating the learner's ability to encode and to decode meaning by recognizing multiple representations of content in situations where the target statements are unmarked. This preempts teaching-to-the-test, and ensures objective and accurate assessment of learning outcomes. At the core of MERLO is a battery of reusable on-line databases that encode the conceptual content of the instructional material. *Each database is for a specific discipline and a specific content*, and is based on a detailed concept mapping of the specific content area (example of 'interactive concept map visualizations', see: Sumner et al., 2005).

Informal disciplines in corporate training, that comprise the majority of content areas, concept mapping is a challenging activity in preparation of instructional material for a workshop or a course. Unlike formal disciplines (e.g., mathematics; engineering), where various versions of concept mapping are readily available in textbooks and other print material, in informal disciplines - such as 'supply management' - concept mapping is often guided by intuition and based on personal experience. It is a process that requires much reflection; re-thinking; recursive refinement; careful separation of semantics from conceptual content; and continuous attention to details. The instructional benefits for corporate training of such investment in concept mapping can hardly be overstated. *Helping the instructor to identify, define, and clarify concepts and procedures in the to-be-learned material results not only in improved delivery of content but - crucially - in enhanced learning outcomes.*

FIRST IMPLEMENTATION (2002): WORKPLACE LEARNING IN COURSE 'RISK MANAGEMENT IN THE SUPPLY CHAIN'

As an integral part of workplace learning program for employees in the early 2000s, Material and Manufacturing Ontario (MMO) Centre of Excellence became interested in exploring the advantages of using digital educational resources for enhancing learning outcomes. The explicit goal was to evaluate the potential of *Meaning Equivalence Reusable Learning Objects (MERLO)* to improve learning outcomes in different contents of current and future workplace workshops and courses in pre-competitive skills (see: Helsper & Eynon, 2010), to be offered jointly by MMO Centre of Excellence and the University of Toronto Innovation Foundation.

Course 'Risk management in the supply chain' was designed and anchored in a detailed concept mapping, conducted by the course instructor with guidance and help of the MERLO team (Shafrir & Krasnor, 2002). Eighty one concepts were identified, carefully formulated, and served as the conceptual content of the course. A MERLO database was constructed for the course, anchored in these concepts, each formulated as a Target Statement (TS). This database was used to guide the delivery of course material to the 20 participants, employed by various material and manufacturing companies in Ontario, and involved continuously with issues related to 'risk management in the supply chain'. In order to evaluate the implementation of MERLO as the core instructional and assessment methodology for the proposed joint training initiative in pre-competitive skills by MMO and the Innovation Foundation of the University of Toronto, our implementation plan included the following 6 steps:

1. Guiding the instructor in conducting detailed concept mapping.
2. Guiding the design of this course based on MERLO formative assessment items.
3. Offering the course to 20 members of the Ottawa-Carlton Manufacturers Network (OCMN); of these, 18 participants were supply management specialists employed by member companies, and 2 participants were doctoral candidates at the School of Business of Carleton University.
4. Supporting the instructor and monitoring the implementation.
5. Ten MERLO assessment items were used to create self-scoring quizzes for each of the weekly formative tests.
6. Providing individual feedback to participants and follow-up class discussion.
7.

PROOF-OF-CONCEPT OF MERLO IN MMO TRAINING CONTEXT

Results and Evaluation

The nature and method of administration of the self-tests were discussed prior to the beginning of the course. The two main questions were: (i) should the tests be a mandatory part of the course; (ii) should there be, in addition to the self-scoring tests (following individual sessions of the course), a final test that would assess

Table 1. Instructions for MERLO self-test scoring

> This self-test was designed to help you optimize your learning outcomes by identifying misunderstandings about the main concepts covered in this in-depth short course. Each MERLO item in the self-test contains 5 statements; at least 2 out of these 5 statements mean the same thing; however, it is possible that more than 2 statements share equivalent meaning. In each item, please mark all statements that mean the same thing.
>
> Please mark the begin/end times below. Once you have completed the test, send it as an attatchment to uri.shafrir@utoronto.ca. You will then receive an attachment that will allow you to self-score this test in preparation for class discussion during the next session.

the overall students' depth of comprehension at the end of the course. Following several discussions, it was decided that the self-scoring tests would be presented to participants as voluntary activities designed to enhance their learning outcomes. The issue of a final test was left open; eventually, the instructor decided not to administer a final test following the completion of the course. Table 2 shows the number of learners that took advantage of the opportunity to enhance their learning outcomes by marking the self-scoring tests.

As can be seen at Table 1, not all learners rose to the occasion and responded to this opportunity to improve their learning outcomes: the numbers of those who did take the self-scoring tests decreased from a high of 16 (out of 20) for the first session, to only 7 who took the fourth (and last) self-scoring test following the last session of the course. This was unexpected and surprising. We expected that the participants - most of which hold middle and senior-management positions, who are adult learners well versed in corporate training - would have seized the opportunity to enhance their learning outcomes. We also thought that the introductory comments at the beginning of the first session, made by Director of Industrial Engagement at Ontario Centers of Excellence, in which MERLO was introduced as an opportunity for participants to maximize their benefits from this in-depth course, would have create high level of motivation and ensure that the great majority of the participants would have taken advantage of this opportunity. As well, we expected other factors to enhance participants' motivation and interest in the self-scoring tests: emphasis placed by the instructor during the first session on the 'in-depth' nature of the course;

Table 2. Number of learners (out of 20) that responded to the self-scoring tests

Session #	1	2	3	4
Number of learners who took the test	16	13	13	7

the presence of Director, University of Toronto Innovation Foundation in the first two sessions; and last – but not least - the clearly apparent benefits for those who took the tests from the detailed feedback received during class discussions at the beginning of each of the sessions.

Why did only 80% of learners participate in the first self-scoring test, and only 35% in the fourth test? The reasons for this are probably varied; some of these reasons were reflected by casual comments made by participants during the course: *"I budgeted 4 hours per week, for 4 weeks, for this activity; I have no time for extra course-related activities"; "the tests require too much effort"; "I prefer true/false tests"*. However, we believe that, in addition to varied pragmatic reasons and personal styles, there was at least one other important factor, namely, expectations created by previous experience that virtually all participants had in taking corporate training courses. Numerous comments by participants made it clear that, in addition to being present at in-class activities, none had ever been asked to write tests in corporate training workshops and courses. On several occasions participants stated that the only additional activity expected in these courses is the customary "Student Feedback Questionnaire" administered at the end of the course, through which participants are asked to rate quality of instruction and overall satisfaction for the course.

Many participants in the in-depth course 'Risk management in the supply chain' were unprepared for a new instructional methodology that offered them an opportunity to enhance their learning outcomes by taking self-scoring tests, at the cost of investing extra time and effort in course-related learning activities. As can be seen from Table 3, the average time to mark the self-scoring tests varied between 24 and 26 minutes. Thus, the direct time investment in self-scoring the tests was rather small; the more time-consuming activities associated with these tests were: self-reflection following identification of erroneous responses; and clarification of misconceptions. In other words, learning.

Table 3. Mean time (SD) spent on taking and marking the self-scoring tests

Session #	1	2	3
Mean time (SD) to complete a self-scoring test (minutes)	23.9 (9.2)	23.8 (7.3)	25.8 (7.6)

MAIN EXPECTATIONS OF SELF-SCORING TESTS RESULTS

Before describing the results of the self-scoring tests it is helpful to recapitulate the expectations embedded in the rationale underlying MERLO assessment items. Briefly stated, we expected that learners who took the tests, following the self-scoring feedback and class discussions, will:

- Improve *total scores* in subsequent tests.
- Increasing proportion of statements that *were correctly marked for equivalence-of-meaning*.
- Initially lower scores on the two types of misleading statements (*Q2* and *Q3*) in which there is *mismatch between surface similarity and meaning equivalence* than on *TS; than on Q1 and Q4 where no such mismatch exists*.
- Improve scores on Q2 and Q3 in subsequent tests.

The following set of figures shows descriptive statistics for the results of the self-scoring tests taken by most learners following each of sessions #1, #2, and #3. The fourth self-scoring test was taken by a minority of the learners (7 out of 20); consequently, no reliable statistics are available for this test.

Each of self-scoring tests #1, #2 and #3 had 10 MERLO assessment items. Figure 2 shows total cumulate scores (proportion correct) for tests #1, #2, #3. In calculating a total score of a MERLO assessment item, the learner received a score of 1 for each of the 5 statements that was answered correctly.

Since each item contained five statements, the operational definition of 'answered correctly' is that all five statements must be correctly checked or unchecked: *those statements that shared equivalence-of-meaning must be checked by the learner, and those statements that did not encode equivalence-of-meaning must be unchecked.* This is a tough criterion. The learner knew that 'at least 2 (but possibly more than two) statements are equivalent in meaning'. This meant that for each item the learner had to make 5 separate decisions, one for each of the five statements in the item. More specifically, for each statement in the item under consideration the learner had to choose between two options namely, 'check' and 'uncheck'. As we have seen, the first step in the item construction procedure is the inclusion of the Target Statement (TS) that anchors the item-family. Therefore, each item in each of the 3 self-scoring tests included a Target Statement (TS); the result is that each test (with 10 meaning equivalence MERLO items) had exactly ten TS. However, the numbers of *Q1, Q2, Q3* and *Q4* statements per test were determined by preferences of the course instructor,

Figure 2. Mean total scores (proportion correct) for self-scoring tests #1, #2, and #3

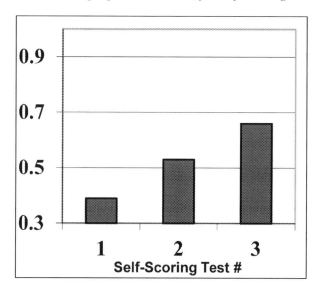

as well as by considerations of item difficulty. As explained above, inclusion of the numbers of *Q2* as well as *Q3* statements increased the level of difficulty of an item, since in these types of statements there is a valence mismatch between surface similarity and meaning equivalence. Inspection of Table 4 shows that in all three tests the total number of *Q2* and *Q3* statements varied slightly between 29 and 30. This rules out the possibility of lower level of item difficulty as an explanation of the pattern of increase of mean total scores across tests #1, #2, and #3.

What, then, might be the interpretation of this clear pattern of consistently increasing total scores across tests (Figure 2)? This upward trend shows improvement in learning. In other words, *learners who consistently took the self-scoring tests, improved their learning outcomes across all MERLO items and across all sessions.*

Table 4. Type and number of statements per quadrant for each test session with 10 MERLO assessment items at MMO

	TS	Q1	Q2	Q3	Q4
Session 1	10	3	17	12	8
Session 2	10	4	17	13	6
Session 3	10	5	12	17	6

Partial Scores of Statements That Share Equivalence-of-Meaning

Positive score is the label for the proportion of correct responses of those statements in each item that *should have been – and, in fact, have been marked - for equivalence of meaning*. These include *TS, Q1* and *Q2* statements. As can be seen in Figure 3, the mean positive scores (SD) increase from 0.78 (0.13) to 0.85 (0.09) to 0.92 (0.09) for tests #1, #2, and #3, respectively. All differences between means are statistically significant ($p<=0.05$).

The interpretation of this upward trend is that learners consistently improved their ability to recognize commonality-of-meaning across *TS* as well as across *Q1* and *Q2* statements, in subsequent tests. We should remember, however, that unlike *TS* and *Q1* statements that 'look similar' and also 'mean the same', *Q2* statements share commonality-of-meaning but 'look different' than target and *Q1* statements.

As stated above, we expect target and *Q1* statements to be easier to recognize as sharing equivalence-of-meaning with *TS* than *Q2* statements. As in the case of total scores detailed above, the upward pattern of partial scores of statements that share equivalence-of-meaning shown in Figure 3 is a clear sign of improved learning across sessions for those learners who chose to take the self-scoring tests.

Figure 3. Mean positive scores (proportion correct) for self-scoring tests #1, #2, and #3

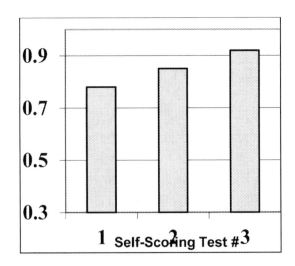

Figure 4. Mean negative scores (proportion correct) for self-scoring tests #1, #2, and #3

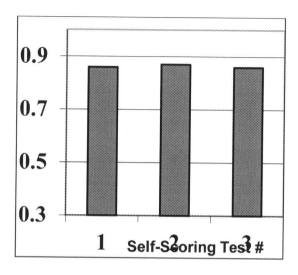

Partial Scores of Statements That do not Share Equivalence-of-Meaning

When Figure 4 is contrasted with the upward trend of positive scores shown in Figure 3, two results become clear from the learner's perspective: first, recognizing statements which share equivalence-of-meaning is a skill that is learnable, and this learning is greatly facilitated by detailed feedback (provided through self-scoring); second, recognizing statements that do not share equivalence-of-meaning is sometime problematic, and remains so even after receipt of detailed feedback.

Partial Scores of *TS, Q1, Q2, Q3,* and *Q4* Statements

Which of the different types of statements were the root cause of these results? Figure 5 shows descriptive statistics for the combined scores of TS and Q1 statements. There are two reasons for combining these scores. The first considers the point of view of the learner who is facing a new item and is scanning the five statements for commonality-of-meaning; since TS and Q1 statements look the same and mean the same, they are practically indistinguishable from the learner's perspective. Second, calculating means and standard deviations separately for Q1 statements is statistically problematic, since the total number of Q1 statements included in each of the three tests is rather small (see Table 4).

Figure 5. Mean combined scores (proportion correct) for (TS+Q1) statements

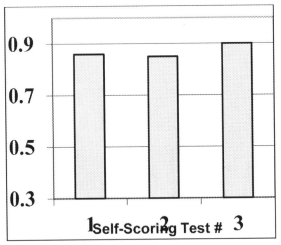

As can be seen the mean scores for (TS + Q1) statements varies between 0.85 and 0.90; there are no significant differences between these scores. In other words, the rather high proportion of correct responses remained the same throughout the three sessions.

Figure 6 shows mean scores (proportion correct) for Q2 statements increasing significantly from 0.71 (0.14) to 0.85 (0.12) to 0.95 (0.09) for tests #1, #2, and #3, respectively. The improvement in learning in Q2 statements across the three self-scoring tests (unlike the high - but stable – scores of (TS + Q1) statements

Figure 6. Mean scores (proportion correct) for Q2 statements

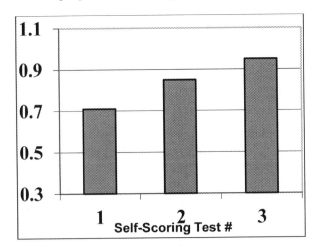

in Figure 5) was anticipated by the pattern of increase in positive scores seen in Figure 3. The tentative conclusion, drawn above, that recognizing statements which share equivalence-of-meaning is a learnable skill, and that this learning is greatly facilitated by detailed feedback (provided through self-scoring), can now be further refined. Specifically, the improvement in learning in *Q2* statements shown in Figure 6 means that learners were successful in learning to separate 'surface similarity' from 'meaning equivalence', which *allowed them to recognize and include in their understanding of a concept statements that 'looked different' but shared meaning with TS*.

Figure 7 shows the mean scores for *Q3* statements (proportion correct), with a small variation in mean scores (proportion correct) in the range 0.82 to 0.84. This pattern, showing no significant improvement across tests, is similar to that in Figure 4 for mean scores of *(TS + Q1)* statements.

This is surprising and in contrast to our expectations stated above. It seems that – unlike the situation with *Q2* statements discussed above – when encountering *Q3* statements learners were quite skilled at separating 'surface similarity' from 'meaning equivalence'. This allowed learners in test #1 to recognize - and exclude from a concept - statements that in spite of 'looking similar' to the target did not share equivalence-of-meaning with it - at the 0.82 level of proportion correct. However, this skill did not improve even with the availability of detailed feedback after self-scoring as the tests progressed. In test #3 the mean score for *Q3* statements was still only 0.84, compare with a mean score for *Q2* statements of 0.95.

Figure 7. Mean scores (proportion correct) for Q3 statements

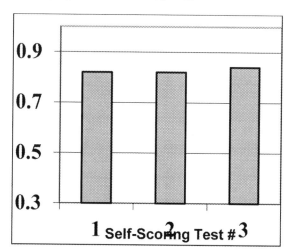

In thinking about the possible reasons for this phenomenon we recall that the great majority of statements in all item-families were represented linguistically; only a few graphically. *This meant that the differences between a Q3 statement and the target were at most in very few words, since the Q3 statement had to 'look similar' to the target. In such situations, a simple strategy of paying close attention in comparing word sequences would reveal non-equivalence-of-meaning between target and Q3 statements.*

Finally, the mean scores (proportion correct) for Q4 statements (Figure 8) are in the range 0.90 to 0.97, somewhat higher than the mean scores for (TS + Q1), Q2, and Q3.

The overall picture emerging from Figures 5 to 8 is that of consistently high proportions of correct responses for target statements as well as for statements from three of the four quadrants: Q1, Q3, and Q4. The only exception are Q2 statements, where the mean scores (proportion correct) monotonically increase from 0.71 to 0.85 to 0.95 in sessions 1, 2, and 3, respectively. This increase is clearly the cause behind the pattern of results observed in Figures 2 to 4, which show increases in both total scores as well as in positive scores, those scores where Q2 statements are implicated across sessions (Figures 2 and 3); while at the same time the negative scores where Q2 statements are not implicated in Figure 5 are stable.

Figure 8. Mean scores (proportion correct) for Q4 statements

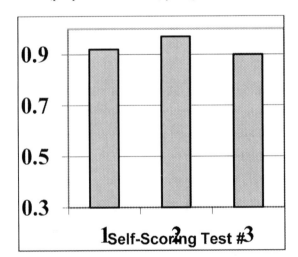

Learners' Evaluation of MERLO

In addition to the ten items that were designed to test deep comprehension of the conceptual content of the last session, test #4 included an additional section in which learners were asked to rate, in detail, their experience with MERLO gained through the self-scoring tests in this course.

Instructions for rating various aspects of the learner's own experience with MERLO self-scoring tests were:

- The self-tests in this course were designed to help you identify misunderstandings of various aspects of some of the core concepts related to "Risk management in the supply chain". Our experience shows that once the learner is provided with detailed feedback regarding misleading aspects of statements (such as mismatches between "the way it looks" and "what it means"), such misunderstandings can be corrected and a deeper level of comprehension of the course material achieved. In the following brief questionnaire we ask you to provide us with feedback on how well these self-tests worked for you. Please mark your answer by typing X next to one of the digits following each question according to this response scale:

1 = not at all 2 = a little 3 = so-so 4 = yes 5 = very much so

- Please use additional space following the questions to comment on the quality of the learning experience in this course. Thank you for your cooperation.

In view of the small number (7 out of 20) of learners' responses to test #4, no reliable descriptive statistics is available. Therefore, all numerical responses to this test are presented in Table 5. In addition, all of the learners' specific comments are reproduced - in their entirety - in Table 6. The numerical scores and the great majority of the learners' comments reveal clear understanding of:

- MERLO instructional and assessment methodology
- recognition of the facilitating role played by the self-scoring tests in clarifying misconceptions and enhancing learning outcomes
- appreciation of the considerable effort invested by the course instructor and the MERLO team in putting together the MERLO infrastructure for this course

Table 5. Learners' responses to questionnaire on the impact of MERLO on learning outcomes

Question / Student	a	b	c	d	e	f	g	Total	Mean
1 Did you find the self-tests useful?	5	4	4	5	4	4	3	29	4.14
2 Was self-scoring helpful?	4	4	4	3	4	4	4	27	3.86
3 Did you use the self-scoring feedback to clarify misunderstandings?	4	5	4	4	3	4	4	28	4.0
4 Were the class discussions and feedback on the self-tests useful?	4	5	3	4	4	5	4	29	4.14
5 Did your learning outcomes improve as the course progressed through the four sessions?	5	4	4	4	5	3	4	29	4.14
6 Are you happy with the level of understanding of the material that you achieved in this course?	5	4	4	5	4	4	4	30	4.29
7 Would you like to see this type of self-tests in future MMO courses and workshops?	4	4	4	4	4	4	2	26	3.71
Total	31	30	27	29	28	28	25	--	--
Mean	**4.43**	**4.29**	**3.86**	**4.14**	**4.0**	**4.0**	**3.57**	--	**4.03**

CONCLUSION

Better Competitiveness of the Mining and Manufacturing Ontario (MMO) Through Enhanced Learning Outcomes

Meaning Equivalence Reusable Learning Object (MERLO) is the core of the novel pedagogy for conceptual thinking for deep comprehension in any content area (Etkind, Kenett & Shafrir, 2016; Shafrir & Krasnor, 2002). Unlike traditional assessment methods such as multiple-choice, problem solving, and short essays that often test memory-for-a-text (or a lecture) and the application of well-rehearsed rules and algorithms learned in training workshops, MERLO evaluates the trainee's *depth of understanding* of newly acquired concepts and skills. MERLO was developed and tested by a team of psychologists, educators, linguists and designers at the Ontario Institute for Studies of Education of the University of Toronto, since the onset of digital reality at the early 2000s. At the core of MERLO is a battery of reusable

Table 6. Learners' comments on their personal experience with ME™ self-scoring tests

* I was a little confused by the integration of this type of testing in the class at first (either I didn't read and understand it well enough prior to tasking the course and/or the course briefing was too vague). But having experienced this testing method, I did feel more comfortable with it as I progressed and it did help to entrench some of the l lesson material in my thought processes.
* Thank you for the time and effort you put into trying to help me learn. I enjoyed the course and the methodology. I believe I got a lot out of the self-test methodology - but is there another self-test format that can give me as much and be easier to put in place. I wish I could give you some feedback on this but I have no experience or basis of comparison. This is the only business course I have taken where self-testing was done. I liked it. Thanks and I hope our paths cross again.
* [I would like to see] self-test yes, whether this type or another. I understand it was hell putting this together.
* [My learning outcomes improved] up until this last test at least. Was it as a result of improved learning or a better understanding of the learning technique? I believe the forced studying the self-tests called for helped the learning experience. The thought that had to be put into many of the questions enhanced the learning experience.
* [the class discussions and feedback on the self-test were useful] – but I found on those statements where I still had issue after getting the feedback it was more a question of semantics in getting a right or wrong answer as opposed to content. (There were not too many of these). Going through the statements in class was a nice review of the previous week's material.
* I usually found the errors of my ways upon reviewing the correct responses.
* I found [the self-tests] to really enhance the learning experience. It made you put thought into the content well after the class, re-enforcing what was learnt in class. The repetition of the content with 'same meaning statements' and subtle differences between a few of the other statements really forced thinking about the issue. This helped learning the content.
* I am not sure if I would want to see this type of self-test used again because I am not convinced that there are any advantages to this methodology for self testing over traditional methods and if there are any advantages whether or not the effort in putting together the various questions by the Instructor warrants its use over others.

on-line databases, each containing item-families that cover both the conceptual content as well as practical skills in a specific content area. MERLO assessment procedures – both self-tests as well as more formal exams - are created on-line by trained instructors; post-test scoring algorithms provide the trainee with immediate and accurate feedback that points out weaknesses and suggests ways of reinforcing sub-optimal skills. MERLO-based feedback drives learning, thus optimizing the acquisition of new knowledge and skills and enhancing training outcomes.

This proof-of-concept demonstrate that different areas in the mining and manufacturing sector, such as: flexible manufacturing; supply management; inventory control; customer service; protection and leveraging of intellectual property; can benefit from workplace training by providing individual companies with practical and cost-effective training solutions through the use of Pedagogy for Conceptual Thinking and Meaning Equivalence Reusable Learning Objects (MERLO).

SECOND IMPLEMENTATION (2003-2004): EXCELLENCE IN MATHEMATICS AND SCIENCE TEACHING AND LEARNING IN HIGH SCHOOL

Excellence in Mathematics and Science Teaching/Learning Consortium was initiated by Adult Study Skills Clinic at Ontario Institute for Studies in Education and University of Toronto Innovation Foundation (UTIF) in 2002. The goal was improving the quality of learning experience and learning outcomes in math and science of young learners in elementary and high schools. The first initiative undertaken by the Consortium was establishing and funding *Meaning Equivalence Design Studio*, a collaborative project between UTIF and Ioffe Physico-Technical Institute of the Russian Academy of Sciences in St. Petersburg. Lyceum Physical-Technical High School was established in 1988 by the Ioffe Institute with the goal of providing mathematical and scientific education of the highest standards to talented adolescents in the St. Petersburg region in Russia. The Lyceum teaching faculty was drawn from mathematicians, physicists, biologists and chemists at several universities and research institutions of the Russian Academy of Sciences in St. Petersburg. Lyceum became renown as a unique educational institution, with students that consistently win international competitions in mathematics and science, and graduates that go on to become well known researchers in their fields.

Meaning Equivalence Design Studio at St. Petersburg was established as the hub of the implementation of *Meaning Equivalence Reusable Learning Objects (MERLO)* in Russia, with the following initial goals:

- Provide teachers and students at the Lyceum with direct access to MERLO methodology, and facilitate its implementation across the math and science curriculum.
- Accumulate Russian expertise, and channel it to teaching mathematics and science to classrooms in Canada and US.

The main vehicle for fulfilling these goals was the joint construction, by Canadian and Russian mathematicians, scientists, and educators, of discipline-specific Meaning Equivalence Reusable Learning Objects (MERLO) databases that encode the conceptual content, by grade-level, of the Lyceum curriculum in mathematics, physics, and biology; and the administration of formative self-scoring tests in order to enhance learning outcomes across the mathematics and science curriculum.

MERLO databases were used in one of two basic modes:

- **Instruction-Support Mode:** Learners had access to self-tests where the conceptual content of learned material was represented in a variety of sign

systems; following completion of a self-test, they receive a self-scoring code, detailed mappings of individual levels of conceptual understanding, and feedback regarding individual, specific aspects of concepts that need refreshing and reinforcement. These issues were then elaborated in follow-up class discussions.
- *Formative assessment* of depth of comprehension of the conceptual content of newly acquired knowledge. The use of alternative sign systems to represent knowledge allow learners to *demonstrate mastery of newly acquired concepts.*

Overview of Meaning Equivalence Design Studio at St. Petersburg

The initial phase of this project was the first of three 2-day workshops for faculty members teaching mathematics, physics, and biology at the Lycee in St. Petersburg, conducted during January 2003.

Lycee faculty MERLO team included:

Mathematics: Valerii Rizhik, PhD; Alexey Zarembo; Konstantin Stolbov
Physics: Michael Ivanov, PhD; Nikolay Khimin, PhD; Andrei Minarsky
Biology: Tatiana Ivanova, PhD; Ludmila Amosova, PhD
Translation and interpretation (Russian/English): Tatiana Eliseeva

Initial Implementation in Spring Semester (January – June 2003)

The first implementation in the Spring Semester (January, 2003) included:

- **Concept Mapping:** Formulating Concept Statements for different concepts, followed by construction of eight MERLO databases, one for each for the 8 courses taught by the eight domain experts.
- Monthly self-scoring formative MERLO assessments in each class/discipline, followed by class discussions of misunderstandings and conceptual 'soft-spots'.
- On-going construction of self-scoring MERLO tests for each discipline, by grade level, for future use.

Construction of MERLO Database for a Course

As part of the workshop activities (Table 7), each of the 8 teachers developed MERLO databases for each of their courses, following the six different types of MERLO items shown in Table 8.

Our experience has shown that inclusion of statements from quadrant Q1 makes a MERLO item too easy, because it gives away the shared meaning due to the valence-match between surface similarity and meaning equivalence - a strong indicator of shared meaning between a Q1 and TS. Therefore, Q1 statements are excluded from MERLO assessment items, as shown in Table 8.

MERLO instructor's template include 3 X 2 table (Figure 9) with six rectangular parts. *Concept Statement* (upper left) include lexical label or definition of the concept; and 5 locations marked A; B; C; D; and E for statements TS; Q2; Q3; and Q4.

Table 7. Workshop 1 activities

Day	Topic
1	MERLO theory
2	MERLO methodology
3	Concept mapping: Theory & practice
4	Concept Statement; Target Statement (TS); quadrant statements (Q2; Q3; Q4)
5	Construction of different item types
6	Construction of MERLO assessment items

Table 8. Numbers of TS; Q2; Q3; Q4 statements per quadrant for each item type

Item type	TS	Q2	Q3	Q4	Total with meaning equivalence (TS+Q2)
I	1	2	2	-	3
II	1	2	1	1	3
III	1	2	-	2	3
IV	1	1	2	1	2
V	1	1	1	2	2
VI	1	3	1	-	4

Figure 9. Instructor's template for MERLO assessment item (physics; Dr. Khimin)

ITEM TYPE I	INSTRUCTOR'S TEMPLATE	
Concept Statement Air humidity	**A [ ]** TS Relative air humidity φ is the ratio of the water vapor partial pressure over the saturated vapor pressure at given temperature	**1. B [ ]** Q2 a. $\varphi = P/P_o$
C [ ] Q2 $\varphi = (P/P_o) \cdot 100\%$	**D [ ]** Q3 Air humidity is the ratio of the water vapor partial pressure over the saturated vapor pressure at given tempetature	**E [ ]** Q3 Relative air humidity is the ratio of the water vapour partial pressure over the air pressure at given temperature

MERLO database include 12 different MERLO assessment items that covered the conceptual content of the course, with 6 MERLO items for weekly quizzes, and 6 MERLO items for the final exam.

Weekly quizzes included:

- Projection of MERLO on screen in front of the class, relevant to the conceptual content of the class during the current week
- Small group discussions
- Class discussion
- Proposed changes to clarify specific MERLO statements

Final exam included, in addition to traditional items, also 6 MERLO assessment items that covered the conceptual content of the course.

Table 9 shows template that specify 12 MERLO items, each with 5 statements, including one TS plus four statements from quadrants Q2; Q3; and Q4; randomly placed in locations A; B; C; D; E. It includes two of each of the 6 different types of MERLO item (Table 8), in random order. *A second workshop in June, 2003* had the following program:

- Extensive reviews of MERLO databases in the different disciplines/grade levels.
- Review of the initial implementations in mathematics, physics, and biology courses by grade level.
- Plans for future MERLO database construction.
- Review of English translations of MERLO assessment items.

Table 9: Template for 12-item MERLO assessment

MERLO	Type/Location	A	B	C	D	E
1	I	Q2	TS	Q3	Q3	Q2
2	V	TS	Q2	Q4	Q4	Q3
3	II	Q3	Q4	Q2	TS	Q2
4	VI	TS	Q2	Q3	Q2	Q2
5	III	Q2	Q2	TS	Q4	Q4
6	I	Q2	Q3	Q3	Q2	TS
7	IV	TS	Q3	Q3	Q2	Q4
8	III	Q4	Q2	Q4	TS	Q2
9	V	Q2	TS	Q4	Q3	Q4
10	VI	Q3	Q2	Q2	TS	Q2
11	IV	Q4	Q3	TS	Q3	Q2
12	II	Q3	Q4	Q2	Q2	TS

Lycee Implementation During Fall Semester (September – December, 2003)

In regular administration at the Lycee in St. Petersburg of monthly self-scoring MERLO assessment items in math, physics and biology courses, students were asked to follow instruction 1 (Figure 10, upper left cell) and mark those statements (at least 2) who share equivalence-of-meaning, then to formulate their description of the concept/reasons *not in writing,* but in the *follow-up class discussion* of misunderstandings and conceptual 'soft-spots'.

Figure 10. Student's MERLO assessment item (physics; Dr. Khimin)

Instructions: At least 2 of these 5 statements – but possibly **more** than 2 – share equivalence-of-meaning. 1 Mark all statements that share equivalence-of-meaning. 2 Briefly describe the concept/reasons you had in mind that guided you in making these decisions.	**A [ ]** $\varphi = P/P_0$	**B [ ]** Relative air humidity φ is the ratio of the water vapor partial pressure over the saturated vapor pressure at given temperature
C [ ] Relative air humidity is the ratio of the water vapour partial pressure over the air pressure at given temperature	**D [ ]** Air humidity is the ratio of the water vapor partial pressure over the saturated vapor pressure at given temperature	**E [ ]** $\varphi = (P/P_0) \cdot 100\%$

In September, 2003, Lycee organized *Meaning Equivalence Olympiad* for several high schools in St. Petersburg, including exhibition of entries of MERLO item-families in mathematics, physics, and biology, composed by students in all grade levels, with announcement of winning entries and awards of prizes in public ceremonies at the Lycee. At the end of the Fall Semester (January, 2004), the two final workshops were held, with the following agenda:

- Extensive reviews of the MERLO in the different disciplines.
- Review of the recent implementation in mathematics; physics; and biology courses.
- Methodological perspectives: Optimizing and fine-tuning item-families.
- Discipline-specific perspectives: Generalizing our experience.
- Plans for future MERLO databases construction.
- Review of English translations of MERLO assessment items.

CONCLUSION

Monthly reports of teachers describe intense student interest and involvement in MERLO class activities, include the following issues/comments:

- Significant number of misunderstandings of Q2 and Q3 statements that include multiple sign systems, i.e., language; formulas; diagrams.
- MERLO assessments are more difficult than regular tests.
- Some MERLO items raised more questions and provoked intense disagreements among students in class discussions.
- Students were aware of 'meaning equivalence' issues; for example, some said "they had seen the world of physics from the other side".
- Teacher's comment: "Students separated to those for whom 'everything was obvious' and the others for whom 'nothing was clear'.
- Disagreements and long class discussions of interpretations of 'equivalence-of-meaning'; teacher's comment: "In two items students disagreed with my interpretation of meaning equivalence".
- "As it was planned, the work was more training/learning than testing. Some tasks were objectively complicated for the 9th grade. Therefore, the questions (also during the test) were about intricate objects – second-order curves and vector equalities. Since no explanations were required in the test, students freely used their qualitative reasons while answering the questions".

Table 10. List of mathematical concepts in ILC MERLO databases for grades 9 - 12

Acceleration
Chain Rule, Change, Composition of two functions, Critical point
Decreasing function, Derivative, Differentiation, Displacement, Distance
Exponent
First derivative, Function
Hyperbolic curve
Implicit differentiation, Increasing function, Inner function
Limit, Local maximum, Local minimum
Outer function
Point of inflection, Power rule, Product Rule
Quotient Rule
Rate, Rate of change
Second derivative, Slope, Slope at a point, Slope of the tangent
Tangent
Velocity

Summery outcomes at the end of 2003 - the first year of implementation are:

- Ongoing, effective communication between the MERLO team and teachers through detailed weekly e-mail progress reports in Russian and English, and three workshops at the Lycee at the beginning, middle, and end of the first year of the project, were instrumental and contributed significantly to the MERLO project success.
- Most students showed significant improvement of their understanding of 'meaning equivalence' during the semester.
- Complete documentation of the project in detailed, regularly distributed reports, including videotaping and transcriptions of all workshops and Olympiad, kept all participants interested and up-to-date.

THIRD IMPLENENTATION (2006): INDEPENDENT LEARNING CENTER (ILC) MATHEMATICS COURSES IN GRADES 9 – 12

Independent Learning Center (ILC) of TVOntario provide an alternative source of public education. ILC is complementary and equivalent to public high school in delivering credit courses in grades 9 – 12 to Ontario learners who did not finish all the courses and therefore did not graduate from high school, and provide student support with technology-enhanced education using new media.

In November, 2006, ILC Director Sarah Irwin invited the Meaning Equivalence Reusable Learning Objects (MERLO) team at Knowledge Media Design Institute (KMDI), Ontario Institute for Studies in Education of University of Toronto, to deliver workshops to ILC management and mathematics teaching faculty, on 'ILC-MERLO Pilot Project Overview'.

This was followed by a program of training ILC mathematics teaching faculty in implementing MERLO pedagogy, including development of MERLO databases for mathematics courses offered at ILC. MERLO databases were developed for ILC courses in mathematics for grades 9 – 12, for the concepts shown in Table 10.

Each MERLO item is focused on a specific mathematics concept, and include several files *with the same Concept Statement, but with a different Target Statement, i.e., TS1; TS2; TS3;* etc. (see example in *Table 11*), and *can be used by teachers to generate different MERLO assessment items (see: Figure 16 for the concept 'Limits')*. It also includes a list of relevant concepts for grading the *student's description of the concept/reasons that guided her in making these decisions.*

Table 11. Examples of MERLO statement TS1, and different alternative statements Q2, Q3, Q4 for Concept Statement 'Power Rule'.

Concept Statement: Power Rule. If n is a rational number and x is a variable, then the derivative of $f(x) = x^n$ is $f'(x) = nx^{n-1}$.

TS1: $\dfrac{d}{dx}\left[x^n\right] = nx^{n-1}$

Q_2: The derivative of x^n is nx^{n-1}.

Q_2: nx^{n-1} is the slope of the tangent at any point $(x, f(x))$ on the curve $y = x^n$.

Q_2: nx^{n-1} is the limiting value of the slopes of a sequence of secants on the curve $y = x^n$.

Q_2: nx^{n-1} is the instantaneous rate of change of x^n at any point on the graph of $y = x^n$

Q_2: $\lim\limits_{h \to 0} \dfrac{(x+h)^n - x^n}{h} = nx^{n-1}$

Q_3: $\dfrac{d}{dx}\left[x^{n-1}\right] = (n-1)x^{n-2}$

Q_3: $\dfrac{d}{dy}\left[y^n\right] = ny^{n-1}$.

Q_4: $\dfrac{dy}{dx} = y'$

Q_4: $\dfrac{dy}{dx} = \dfrac{dy}{du} \times \dfrac{du}{dx}$

Q_4: $x^n = x\left(x^{n-1}\right)$

Relevant concepts: power rule, derivative, slope, tangent, exponent, limit, differentiation

Following are examples of ILC screen images of students' training in MERO formative self-assessments. Figures 11, 12, 13, and 14 are screen shots of ILC's 'Introduction to MERLO self-tests' and provide students with hands-on experience in gaining better understanding of equivalence-of-meaning of different representations of a concept in various sign systems, of MERLO assessment item. Figures 15, 16, 17, and 18 show a specific example of MERLO self-test sequence for the concept 'Limits', including student response, and followed by feedback to student response. Free access to such MERLO self-tests provide students with opportunities to deepen their level of understanding of the conceptual content in mathematics courses, delivered in-class and online.

CONCLUSION

Pedagogy for Conceptual Thinking With Meaning Equivalence Reusable Learning Objects (MERLO) Enhance Learning Outcomes

This chapter describe the evolution, since early 2000s, of Meaning Equivalence Reusable Learning Objects (MERLO). Guided by the goal of deepening the level of students' conceptual understanding of learned content, it describes in detail MERLO

Figure 11. Welcome to MERLO

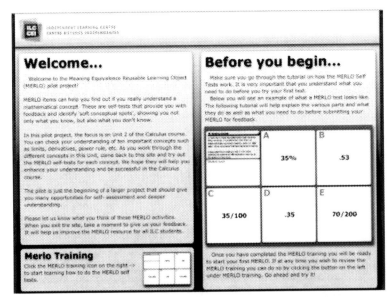

Figure 12. Introduction to MERLO self-tests 1

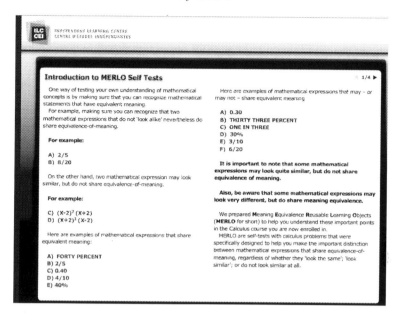

Figure 13. Introduction to MERLO self-tests 2

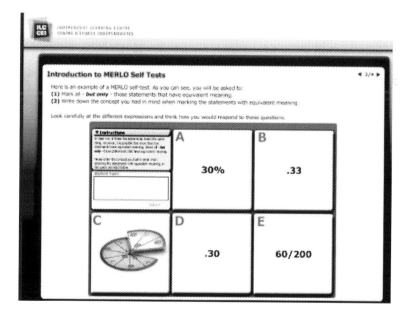

Figure 14. Introduction to MERLO self-tests 3

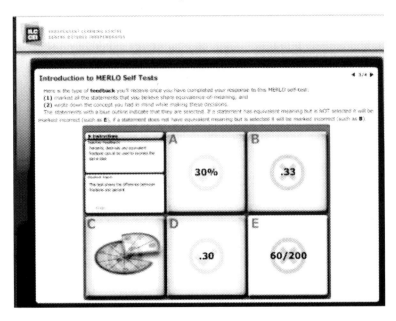

Figure 15. Introduction to concept 'Limits' MERLO item 1

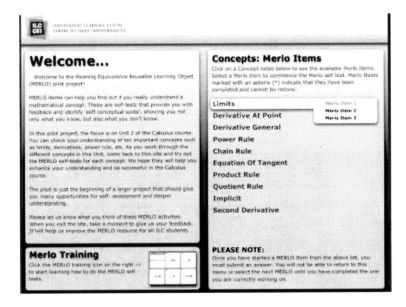

Meaning Equivalence Reusable Learning Objects (MERLO) Access to Knowledge

Figure 16. Concept 'Limits' MERLO item 1

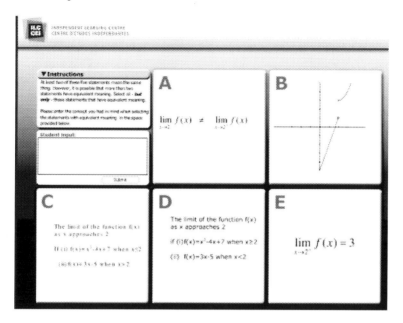

Figure 17. Student response to concept 'Limits' MERLO item 1

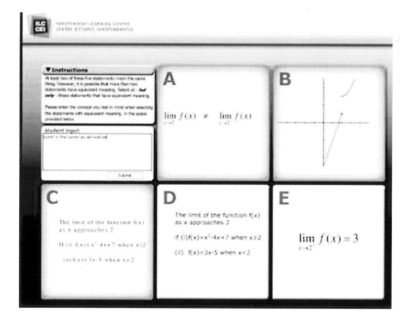

Figure 18. Feedback to student response to concept 'Limits' MERLO item 1

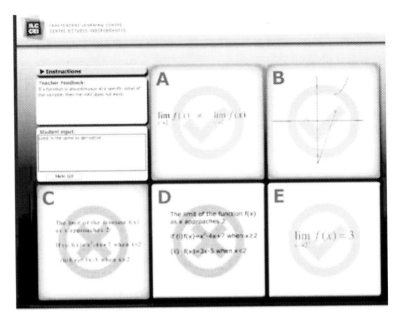

evolution in three different implementations in different knowledge domains, including mathematics, physics, biology, and management, as well as different in-class and online pedagogical activities. Important research findings are:

- Formative MERLO assessments with small group and class discussions, often encourage disagreements among students and arguments about 'meaning equivalence' of different representations of a concept.
- Individual students' online self-tests and feedback, document their level of understanding of specific concepts.
- MERLO assessments document enhanced learning outcomes, and teachers' observations of students' awareness of their level of conceptual understanding.

REFERENCES

Cabre, M. T. (1998). *Terminology: Theory, Methods, and Applications*. Amsterdam: Johns Benjamins Publishing.

Di Giacomo, D., Ranieri, J., & Lacasa, P. (2017). Digital Learning as Enhanced Learning Processing? Cognitive Evidence for New Insight of Smart Learning. *Frontiers in Psychology*, *8*, 1329. doi:10.3389/fpsyg.2017.01329 PMID:28824508

Friedman, R. S., & Deek, F. P. (2003). Innovation and Education in the Digital Age: Reconciling the Roles of Pedagogy, Technology, and the Business of Learning. *IEEE Transactions on Engineering Management*, *50*(4), 403–412. doi:10.1109/TEM.2003.819650

Helsper, E. J., & Eynon, R. (2010). Digital natives: Where is the Evidence? *British Educational Research Journal*, *36*(3), 503–520. doi:10.1080/01411920902989227

Kittredge, R. I. (1983). Sematic Processing of Texts in Restricted Sublanguages. In N. J. Cercone (Ed.), Computational Linguistics (pp. 45-58). Academic Press.

Neumann, M. M., Finger, G., & Neumann, D. L. (2017). A Conceptual Framework for Emergent Digital Literacy. *Early Childhood Education Journal*, *45*(4), 471–479. doi:10.100710643-016-0792-z

Puntambekar, S., & Goldstein, J. (2007). Effect of Visual Representation of the Conceptual Structure of the Domain on Science Learning and Navigation in a Hypertext Environment. *Journal of Educational Multimedia and Hypermedia*, *16*(4), 429–459.

Shafrir, U., & Krasnor. (2002). *Increasing competitiveness of Ontario's material and manufacturing companies through enhanced training outcomes in pre-competitive skills*. Meaning Equivalence Design Studio, Resource Center for Academic Technology, University of Toronto.

Stafford, N. (2010). Science in the Digital Age: The Goals of Science Have Not Changed Since the Early Days of the Lindau Meeting, Yet the Ways They Are Pursued Is. *Nature*, *467*(7317), 14. doi:10.1038/467S19a PMID:20811426

Sumner, T., Ahmad, F., Bhushan, S., Gu, Q., Molina, F., Willard, S., ... Jan'ee, G. (2005). Linking learning goals and educational resources through interactive concept map visualizations. *International Journal on Digital Libraries*, *5*(1), 18–24. doi:10.100700799-004-0112-x

Chapter 3
Enhancing Conceptual Thinking With Interactive Concept Discovery (INCOD)

Masha Etkinda
Ryerson University, Toronto, Canada

Uri Shafrir
University of Toronto, Canada

ABSTRACT

Interactive concept discovery (InCoD), based on concept parsing algorithms (CPA), is a novel learning tool in the context of pedagogy for conceptual thinking. It supports semantic searches of key word in context (KWIC), an interactive procedure that use text analysis (concordance, collocation, co-occurrence, word frequency) and allows students to explore the course knowledge repository (KR) for discovery of conceptual contents. InCoD guides sequential teaching/learning episodes in an academic course by focusing learners' attention on conceptual meaning. InCoD is part of a pedagogical approach that is very different from the usual classroom scenario where students are given a problem-solving exercise and asked to solve it individually.

DOI: 10.4018/978-1-7998-1985-1.ch003

INTRODUCTION

The emergent discipline of concept science is a novel generic methodology for parsing and analyzing concepts, applicable to the various knowledge domains and professions, with tools for recognizing, representing, organizing, exploring, communicating, and manipulating knowledge encoded in controlled vocabularies of sublanguages. Concept science document the evolution of content and structure of concepts and categorization, knowledge representation and use. Certain words, used to describe regularities in human experience, acquire specific meanings that differ from their meanings in the general use of language. These code words are unique names of concepts - patterns in the data, invariants. The use of code words is common practice in all disciplines and in all domains of knowledge. It originates from the common need to eliminate – at least reduce – ambiguity, and to define conceptual content in precise terms that allow clear demarcation between the known and the unknown.

Code words in scholarly discourse are lexical labels of concepts in a controlled vocabulary that encode conceptual content within the body of knowledge in a discipline, a profession, a domain. A lexical label acts as proper name of a regularity, an organizing principle behind a collection of facts in context. Lexical label is often one or more common words (mostly nouns and noun phrases) used to label a recognized pattern in human experience and to communicate a well-defined meaning. Lexical labels of concepts differ from the use of these same words in ordinary language in two important ways:

- Lexical labels of concepts do not encode the literal meanings associated with their constituent words in the common use of the language. Each such label encodes a connoted meaning, rooted in the regularity being considered, that differs from the literal meaning of the word(s).
- Lexical labels of concepts cannot be replaced by synonyms. Each label functions as a proper name of the signified concept.

Initiates – insiders who share the code - know that a lexical label of a concept serves a similar function to that of a proper name, in contrast to 'outsiders' who encounter a lexical label and do not associate it with discipline-specific meaning. They assume that the label is just a word in general language, and therefore may be substituted by a synonym: 'In general language it is easy to find synonymous expressions, but in specialist discourse the exact term for the conceptual equivalent is expected' (Sager, 1993).

METHODOLOGY

Conceptual curation is a recent development in curation of large repositories containing digital full-text documents (Shafrir & Etkind, 2011). It includes the use of semantic searches that reveal structured, multi-layered building blocks of concepts with lateral and hierarchical interactions. Concepts are labeled patterns in the data that encode 'meaning' in different domains of knowledge: semantic content embedded in them by the situation being documented, and the specific constraints associated with data generated during this evolutionary process.

Content of an academic course is encoded in its main concepts, accessible through a comprehensive collection of full-text digital documents. Such a collection is a Knowledge Repository (KR) that may contain all types of relevant digital documents: primary sources; monographs; technical reports; databases (numerical data; images; 3D artifacts; (see: http://research.library.gsu.edu/zotero). KR opens pedagogical horizons to instructors and learners, and shifts the emphasis from memorization of facts to experiential learning with Interactive Concept Discovery (InCoD), that allows exploration of particular conceptual situations from different points of view, in a particular knowledge domain, represented in different ways by a variety of authors of different documents in KR.

InCoD is a novel semantic search tool based on Concept Parsing Algorithms (CPA; Shafrir & Etkind, 2017; see also: http://libguides.usc.edu/textmining/tools; https://voyant-tools.org/). InCoD is a novel learning tool in the context of pedagogy for conceptual thinking (Etkind, Kenett & Shafrir, 2016; Shafrir, & Kenett, 2016). It support semantic searches of Key Word In Context (KWIC), an interactive procedure that use text analysis (concordance; collocation; co-occurrence; word frequency) and allows students to explore the course Knowledge Repository (KR) for discovery of conceptual contents. InCoD guides sequential teaching/learning episodes in an academic course by focusing learners' attention on conceptual meaning. InCoD is part of a pedagogical approach that is very different from the usual classroom scenario where students are given a problem-solving exercise and asked to solve it individually. Pedagogy for conceptual thinking include weekly formative assessments, structured to provide opportunities for students to discuss and exchange ideas; to share and contrast points-of-view; to prompt and refresh each other's memory regarding important details of the conceptual situation; and to 'compare notes' about possible responses. It is an intuitive, interactive procedure that allows the discovery of elements of the building blocks underlying the lexical label of a concept within a particular context, namely, co-occurring sub-ordinate concepts and relations. This procedure guides the user to construct concept maps that clearly identify internal conceptual structure, namely, hierarchical and lateral relations among concepts and their building blocks. A user develop an evolving Individual Index by identifying the lexical label of a particular concept within a context in a discipline; then conducts Key Word In Context (KWIC) semantic searches of this lexical label; evaluates the consistency of appearance of candidate co-occurring concepts and candidate relations among concepts across different documents in KR that contain this lexical label. In successive iterations, the learner:

- Read and annotate found documents, then tag and link them to other relevant documents
- mark and save 'candidate' lexical labels in his/her Individual Index
- Evaluate the degree of relevance of a particular document to the conceptual situation under consideration, and identifies different representations that share equivalence-of-meaning
- Construct concept maps - alternative graphical representations of links between concepts and their building blocks

RESULTS

Sequential stages of development of Individual Index and concept maps become a dynamically updated and comprehensive record of individual learners Interactive Concept Discovery (InCoD) that document the process and outcomes of sequential research and learning episodes. It reveals the learner's consistency of 'drilling down' for discovering deeper building blocks of the particular concept, and shows the temporal evolution of outcomes of the research-and-learning sequence: deeper levels of comprehension of conceptual content. This digital record may be also saved in a learner's e-Portfolio as an authentic, evidence-based demonstration of mastery of knowledge (Shafrir, Etkind, & Treviranus, 2006).

Figure 1 is an example for text analysis of this paper with Voyant Tools (https://voyant-tools.org/). The table at the lower right shows Key Word In Context (KWIC) – CORCORDANCE – of TERM = 'incod', namely, all individual locations in this paper where the word 'incod' appears, including several context words on the left side and several context words on the right side of the word 'incod'. In addition, other visualizations and statistics are available (see relevant documents on the website). Figure 2 shows

Voyant Tools analysis of TERM = 'conceptual' in this paper.

Weekly use of such text analysis tools allows learners to deepen their understanding of specific conceptual contexts in class discussions and weekly formative assessments in the course.

Figure 1. Text analysis of this paper with Voyant Tools Term = 'incod'

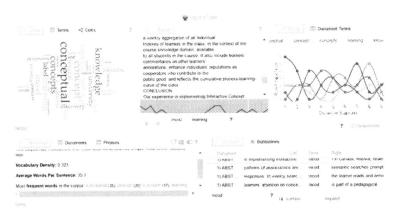

Figure 2. Text analysis of this paper for Term = 'conceptual'

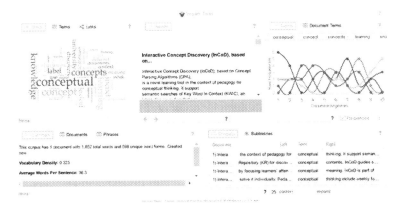

In addition to evolving Individual Indexes, shared between individual students and the course instructor, CONCEPEDIA (Cooperative Conceptual Encyclopedia) is a weekly aggregation of all

Individual Indexes of learners in the class, in the context of the course knowledge domain, available to all students in the course. It also include learners' commentaries on other learners' annotations, enhance individuals' reputations as cooperators who contribute to the public good, and reflects the cumulative process-learning-curve of the class.

CONCLUSION

Our experience in implementing Interactive Concept Discovery (InCoD) in Canada, Russia, Israel, Australia, and Italy, include: Ontario Institute for Studies in Education of University of Toronto (OISE/UT); Roots and Routes Summer Institute, University of Toronto, Scarborough; Faculty of Engineering and Architectural Science at Ryerson University, Toronto; Independent Learning Center (ILC) of TVOntario; Material and Manufacturing Ontario (MMO) Centre of Excellence; Mount Sinai Hospital, Toronto; Russian Academy of Sciences – Lycee, Ioffe Physico-Technical Institute, St. Petersburg; Meir Medical Center, Kfar Saba, Israel; Faculty of Engineering, Ben Gurion University, Israel; School of Education, University of New England, Australia; and M@t.abel, the Italian national mathematics educational program, coordinated academically by the Department of Mathematics at University of Turin. These implementations include workshops for training of instructors, and classroom implementations in several knowledge domains: Language (ESL; learning disabilities); Social Science (psychology; teacher education); History; Architecture; Mathematics (algebra; geometry; statistics); Science (physics; biology); Health; Business (project management; risk management).

A recent OECD Review of 'Evaluation and Assessment in Education: Synergies for Better Learning' (OECD Publishing, 2013) provides strong evidence for the important role of formative assessment in enhancing students' learning outcomes, and notes that 'The quality of formative assessment rests, in part, on strategies teachers use to elicit evidence of student learning related to goals, with the appropriate level of detail to shape subsequent instruction' (Nusche, 2013). Our research shows that students' learning records, including: InCoD-prompted Individual Indexes and CONCEPEDIAS in different courses and knowledge domains, as well as formative assessment outcomes, provide authentic evidence of mastery of knowledge and higher-level thinking (see also: Jefferson & Long, 2008).

REFERENCES

Etkind, M., Kenett, R. S., & Shafrir, U. (2016). Learning in the Digital Age with Meaning Equivalence Reusable Learning Objects (MERLO). In E. Railean, G. Walker, A. Elçi, A., & L. Jackson (Eds.), Handbook of Research on Applied Learning Theory and Design in Modern Education (pp. 310-333). IGI Global.

Jefferson, W., & Long, E. M. (2008). Electronic Portfolio as a Means of Authentic Assessment. In D. Cook & R. L. Sittler (Eds.), Practical Pedagogy for Library Instructors: 17 Innovative Strategies to Improve Student Learning, (pp. 139-146). Chicago, IL: Association of College and Research Libraries.

Nusche, R. (2013). *Student assessment: Putting the learner at the centre. Synergies for Better Learning: An International Perspective on Evaluation. Reviews of Evaluation and Assessment in Education and Assessment*. Paris: OECD Publishing.

OECD. (2013). *Synergies for Better Learning: An International Perspective on Evaluation. Reviews of Evaluation and Assessment in Education and Assessment*. Paris: OECD Publishing.

Sager, J. C. (1993). *Language Engineering and Translation: Consequences of Automation*. Amsterdam: Johns Benjamins Publishing.

Shafrir, U., & Etkind, M. (2011). Conceptual Curation: Certificate Program for Librarians. *Proceedings of International Conference on Education and New Learning Technologies*.

Shafrir, U., & Etkind, M. (2017). Concept Parsing Algorithms (CPA) for Textual Analysis and Discovery. *Emerging Research and Opportunities*. doi:10.4018/978-1-5225-2176-1

Shafrir, U., Etkind, M., & Treviranus, J. (2006). eLearning Tools for ePortfolios. In A. Jaffari & C. Kauffman (Eds.), Handbook of Research on ePortfolios (pp. 206-216). Hershey, PA: Idea Group.

Shafrir, U., & Kenett, R. S. (2016). Concept Science Evidence Based MERLO Learning Analytics. In Handbook of Research on Applied Learning Theory and Design in Modern Education (pp. 334-357). IGI Global. doi:10.4018/978-1-4666-9634-1.ch016

Chapter 4
Teachers Involved in Designing MERLO Items

Ornella Robutti
Università di Torino, Italy

Paola Carante
Università di Torino, Italy

Theodosia Prodromou
University of New England, Australia

Ron S. Kenett
The KPA Group and the Samuel Neaman Institute, Technion, Israel

ABSTRACT

This chapter looks at an in-depth application of meaning equivalence reusable learning objects (MERLO) to mathematics education and teacher professional development. The study has been conducted during professional development courses for in-service teachers and is focused on mathematics teachers' praxeologies, namely their didactical techniques and theoretical aspects embraced to accomplish a task. Specifically, the task given to the teachers consists in designing MERLO items to be used in their classrooms, working in groups or individually, after having been trained by researchers in mathematical education. The chapter presents two case studies with data, one dealing with secondary school teachers in Italy and one concerning primary teachers in Australia. One of the main aims of the study is the analysis of the praxeologies of these teachers when they are engaged in designing MERLO items during professional development programs. The chapter demonstrates, with these examples, the generalizability potential of MERLO items and that they can be used in different cultural and institutional ecosystems.

DOI: 10.4018/978-1-7998-1985-1.ch004

Copyright © 2020, IGI Global. Copying or distributing in print or electronic forms without written permission of IGI Global is prohibited.

INTRODUCTION

A common and recognized world wide challenge is to improve the efficacy and efficiency of teaching, learning and assessing. Teaching the right things in the right way is an important objective for both teachers and education research.

In recent years many studies in different disciplines, including mathematics education, have been carried out with the aim of providing teachers, students and educational systems with new didactical and methodological tools. A collection of research contributions appeared in the Proceedings of the International Commission on Mathematical Instruction, a book fully dedicated to the design task in mathematics education (Margolinas, 2013).

MERLO (Meaning Equivalence Reusable Learning Objects) is an innovative methodological-didactical tool originally introduced by Shafrir and Etkind, and later developed by others, that uses alternative, multi-semiotic, representations in different sign systems to focus the attention of learners on meanings. MERLO allows teachers to assess the depth of understanding of contents, and to enhance students' conceptual thinking (Etkind, Kenett & Shafrir, 2010).

Classroom activities using MERLO can be performed in every subject matter and at different grade levels (e.g. see contributions in other chapters of this book; Etkind, Kenett & Shafrir, 2016; Arzarello, Robutti & Carante, 2015; Robutti et al., in press).

In this chapter, we present the use of MERLO in mathematics education, with a double perspective:

1. Analyze MERLO task design carried out by mathematics teachers of primary and secondary school.
2. Study the practices of these teachers involved in the MERLO task design.

According to the Meta-Didactical Transposition framework (Arzarello et al., 2014), the main aim of this study is to analyse the praxologies of teachers involved in professional development courses that make use of MERLO and engage participants in designing tasks for their students. In order to find similarities and differences between the teachers' praxeologies in designing MERLO for their students, we present two different methodologies: i) the Italian one, which involves mathematics teachers of secondary school, and ii) the Australian one, which involves primary school teachers. In both cases, teachers collaborate together and/or with researchers in mathematics education. As demonstrated in recent studies, working with colleagues and with academics is an important aspect of teachers' professional development (Robutti et al., 2016). The chapter focuses on the design of MERLO items for mathematics teaching, learning and assessment, as part of professional development program.

Teachers' Praxeologies

The purpose of studying teachers involved in a professional development is pursued in this study according to the frame of Meta-Didactical Transposition (Arzarello et al., 2014), which offers an interpretative model of teachers' praxeologies. A praxeology is introduced by Chevallard (1999) in his Anthropological Theory of Didactics, to indicate four interrelated components: task, technique, technology and theory. The given task, and the corresponding technique used to solve the task, are the practical counterpart of the praxeology (the *praxis*), while the technology (in the sense of justification) and the theory are the theoretical counterpart that validates the use of that technique (the *logos*). A mathematical praxeology is made of a task (for example, to find the equation of the tangent to the graph of a generic function f) that the students have to solve, the employed technique and the justification for using it, all within a specific mathematical theory.

At the same time, the teacher's questions and actions used to build such a mathematical praxeology with students constitute a didactical praxeology. What may occur is:

- The teacher introduces students to a type of task (task);
- The teacher manages how to organize such an approach (technique);
- The teacher knows why he/she has to organize it like that (technology);
- The teacher justifies why she/he knows that he/she has to organize it like that (theory).

The Meta-Didactical Transposition framework uses the idea of praxeology at a meta-level, and calls it meta-didactical praxeology, which comprises task, technique, and justifying discourses that develop during the process of teacher professional development. As in the previous case, what may occur is:

- The teachers are introduced to a task;
- The teachers use a technique to solve it;
- The teachers know why they choose such solution;
- The teachers justify technique and technology with a theory.

A typical example is when the new praxeology is developed in response to changes in the official curriculum or in external assessment expectations for students. Simultaneously, the researchers' praxeologies also evolve as a consequence of their interaction with the teachers and from their reflections on their experiences of the educational programme.

Evolution in the praxeologies does not mean that all the teachers involved in the educational program evolve in the same way with the same transformation of components; different teachers may evolve in different ways, with respect to their history and experience. The meta-didactical praxeologies of the two communities of teachers and researchers change with respect to the institutional environment in which they reside. We focus on the meta-didactical praxeologies of primary and secondary school teachers, who are involved in professional development courses that present MERLO as a new didactical-methodological tool. Specifically, the teachers collaborate with a community of researchers in mathematics education to accomplish the task of designing MERLO items for teaching, learning and assessing mathematics in their classrooms.

MERLO Framework

MERLO (Meaning Equivalence Reusable Learning Object) is a didactical and methodological tool introduced by Etkind and Shafrir (Etkind, Kenett, & Shafrir, 2010), for investigating students' deep understanding of concepts through both formative and summative assessments. The first use of MERLO has been in architecture (Etkind & Shafrir, 2013), but then it was adapted for several other knowledge areas (Shafrir & Kenett, 2016), including mathematics and mathematics education (Arzarello, Robutti & Carante, 2015).

The versatility of the tool is due to its main features: a MERLO item consists of five statements (sentences, graphical representations, pictures, diagrams, tables, etc.) that may or may not share meaning. One of the five statements is the Target Statement (TS), which encodes different features of a particular concept within a specific discipline. The other four statements are linked to the Target Statement by two different criteria: 1) the statement may or may not share meaning with TS (Meaning Equivalence criterion); 2) the statement may or may not have a surface similarity with TS (Surface Similarity criterion).

In mathematics education, the first criterion of *Meaning Equivalence* can be interpreted as "a common mathematical meaning across several representations", like for example the algebraic expression of a parabola and the corresponding graph in a Cartesian plane, or the parabola appearing in some real life situations. The second criterion of *Surface Similarity* designates "representations that look similar", which means that they are similar in appearance, due to similar formal elements (perhaps the same register, as defined by Duval, 2006), but they have different meanings, like for example the algebraic expressions $(a+b)^2$ and a^2+b^2.

Based on these two criteria, it is possible to create statements within MERLO items that have different roles in relation to TS: they are presented in Table 1 with their labels (Q2, Q3, Q4).

According to the Table 1, each statement within a MERLO item can be:

- Q2 if it represents the same mathematical concept in another register than TS (it has a relation of Meaning Equivalence with TS) and it is connected in the meaning with TS;
- Q3 if it represents another concept in the same register of TS (it has a relation of Surface Similarity with TS) and acts as distractor;
- Q4 if it represents another concept in another register than TS (it has neither Meaning Equivalence, nor Surface Similarity with TS) and acts as distractor.

A MERLO item is made of five statements, of which one is TS, at least one is Q2, and the others are Q3 or Q4. The students that correctly solve the MERLO item mark only TS and the Q2 statements, and justify their choice with arguments.

The number of each type of statement (Q2, Q3, Q4) may be different from one item to another, only TS is unique. This categorization of the statements is useful in the design phase, but it is removed from the MERLO item before it is administered to the students who are asked to solve it.

Figure 1 (Carante & Robutti, 2016) shows an example of MERLO item in the teacher/designer version, where the statements are labeled with TS and Q2, Q3, and Q4. The TS and the two Q2 are connected by the Meaning Equivalence criterion, but they do not have a Surface Similarity: the TS and the two Q2 deal with the mathematical relation of inverse proportionality that is represented using different modalities and registers (symbolic relation in A, verbal definition in B, graphs in a Cartesian plane in C). The Q3 only has a Surface Similarity with the TS, because it represents a similar symbolic relation between the same quantities x and y that are not inverse proportional. The Q4 satisfies neither the Meaning Equivalence nor the Surface Similarity criteria with the TS: it shows a graph with two quantities X and Y that do not satisfy the inverse proportional relation.

The task for the solvers consists in:

Table 1. Statements with different roles related to a TS

	Meaning Equivalence with TS	*Surface Similarity* **with TS**
Q2	YES	NO
Q3	NO	YES
Q4	NO	NO

Figure 1. MERLO item about inverse proportionality (teacher/designer version)

Inverse proportionality	TS	Q2
1. Mark the statements (at least two) that share the same mathematical meaning. 2. Write the reasons that guided you in the choice.	A [ ] $y = \dfrac{k}{x}$ k constant	B [ ] Two inversely proportional quantities X and Y have fixed product
Q2	**Q3**	**Q4**
C [ ] (graphs of $f(x)=\tfrac{1}{x}$, $g(x)=\tfrac{3}{x}$, $h(x)=\tfrac{8}{x}$)	D [ ] $y = \dfrac{k}{x^2}$ k constant	E [ ] (scatter plot with k=2)

1. marking all the statements (two or more, not knowing how many) in multiple representations that share the same mathematical meaning (in this case inverse proportionality namely A, B, and C).
2. justifying their choice with arguments (the fact that in A there is a family of functions that represent two inverse proportional quantities, in B there is the definition of two quantities that are inverse proportional, and in C there are particular cases of inverse proportional quantities).

The formulation of the task, even if substantially equal in all the examples appearing in literature, can be different in using words: in this MERLO item we are referring to the formulation of task that is used and shared in Italy.

Research Aim and Question

The research aim of this chapter consists in studying the evolution of teachers' praxeologies when they design MERLO items for their classes at (i) secondary school level in Italy, and (ii) primary school level in Australia, in collaboration with researchers in mathematics education affiliated at their respective Universities (authors of this chapter). The main research question in this study is: "Are there any similarities and/or differences in the teachers' praxeologies when designing MERLO items, working with two methodologies?" We are expecting differences due to the different institutional contexts where the experiences have been conducted, but we are also expecting some similarities that link the final praxeologies of the teachers when designing MERLO items.

METHODOLOGY

The Italian secondary school teachers initially approached the MERLO items through research papers (Etkind, Kenett & Shafrir, 2010; Etkind & Shafrir, 2011; 2013) and examples coming from the previous experience in using them in education. First of all, the teachers attended a seminar by Kenett as part of their professional development course. Secondly, they were engaged in the solution and discussion of some MERLO items designed earlier by a Russian community of teachers who designed and used MERLO items previously.

The Italian teachers of this study were asked to solve the MERLO items designed by the Russian teachers and to discuss their understanding of MERLO items, from the mathematical and pedagogical point of view. Then, they were asked to design new MERLO items for secondary school mathematics classrooms in Italy, starting from an institutional context, namely questions appeared in the Italian national assessment tests (INVALSI) of previous years. The teachers worked in small groups both in the same location, and also at a distance (through a platform).

The Australian primary teachers were also provided with research papers (Arzarello, Robutti & Carante, 2015; Arzarello et al. 2015; Robutti at al., 2016) about MERLO items and their important role in education as teaching and assessment tools. They were further provided with a recorded lecture about constructing the different statements of a variety of MERLO items and some examples of MERLO items. Then, they were asked to design a MERLO item that could be used to assess students' understanding of the learning outcomes across a sequence of three lesson plans. During the completion of their MERLO item, teachers shared their ideas on the online forum, they discussed the appropriateness of their MERLO statements with the other teachers and the researcher affiliated at the University. When they completed the MERLO item, the teachers took a screenshot of their MERLO items and they were required to explain their design strategies and justify the sequence of the steps they took to construct their MERLO item to assess their students' understanding of specific concepts.

The data of this chapter consists of MERLO items designed by the teachers, video recordings of the teacher face-to-face meetings, texts by the platform (uploaded files and interventions in the forum), namely the content related to the productions of items and the explanations and justifications of the steps they followed to design them.

The authors of this chapter watched all video recordings and analyzed the transcribed data including coding teachers' discussion on the online forum. The Italian data included the intermediate and final MERLO items designed by a small group of 3 teachers, and the discussion developed by the 3 teachers to a big group of 7 teachers. These data have been analyzed in terms of the process of designing the statements, looking at those statements that remained the same, versus those statements that changed - during the various formulations of the item - in parallel to the supporting discourse of the teachers. The observed process of design includes the different versions of a MERLO item, along with the discourse justifying the changes or the maintenance of a statement, motivated by institutional or mathematical reasons. The product of design is the final version of the item, and our analysis concentrates on the observation of the corresponding process over time.

The analysis of those statements that change or not in the MERLO items provide us with insights into the praxis – namely, the practical components of the praxeologies of the teachers as designers of items. Teachers' face-to-face discussions, as well as on-line discussions, provide us with insights into the logos - that is: the theoretical components of teachers' praxeologies.

The Australian data included the final versions of MERLO items designed by all the 286 teachers and the discussions developed by them in the on-line forum. These data have been analyzed in terms of the process of designing the statements, looking at the justifying discourse reported by the teachers on their production of one item, for supporting their choices on each statements, and motivated by institutional or mathematical reasons. The product of design is the final version of the item, and our analysis concentrates on the observation of the corresponding process over time.

The Evolution Of The Italian Secondary School Teachers' Praxeologies When Designing Merlo Items

This section analyses an example of MERLO item designed by the Italian team of mathematics secondary school teachers, working in collaboration with mathematics education researchers affiliated with the University of Turin.

The data selection presents two versions of the same MERLO item (version V1 in Fig. 3; version V2 in Fig. 4), in which statements change over time. They are complemented with some excerpts quoted from a face-to-face discussion among teachers and researchers, as a shift from version V1 to version V2. Following this progress, we aim at outlining the associated evolution of the Italian secondary school mathematics teachers' praxeologies when designing MERLO items for teaching, learning and assessing. The example is constructed around the issue of frequencies distribution and belongs to the main topic of "data and forecasts", one of the basic standards in mathematics both in the Italian curriculum and all over the world. As pointed out by some teachers' comments during the face-to-face meeting, the starting point for designing the MERLO item has been a question from the National Assessment test in Italy, called INVALSI. The question appearing in Fig. 2 (INVALSI, 2012) provided the idea to design a statement in form of a diagram that represents the frequencies distribution of children by age.

Teachers Involved in Designing MERLO Items

Figure 2. Original test questions from INVALSI, 2012

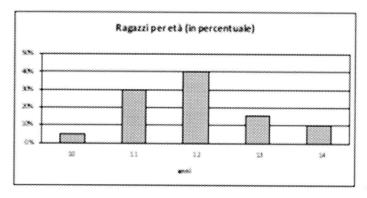

Figure 3. MERLO item about frequencies, version V1

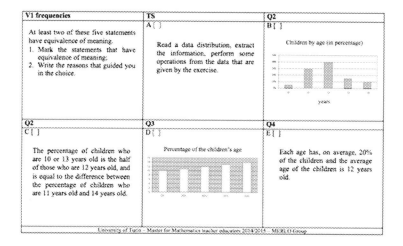

Figure 4. MERLO item about frequencies, version V2

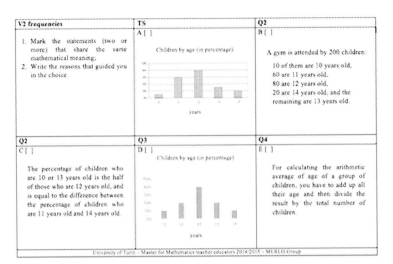

Teachers' comments: *The target statement in V1 has a precise task and looks like an exercise. At the beginning of the experience, we started from an INVALSI question for designing this MERLO item. Then, we changed the precise task in the TS in V2. Another change appears in a Q2 statement: during the last meeting my colleague and I added a new Q2 statement (that one in B in the version V2). We simply applied the percentages in the graph to a group of 200 people. It consists in a simple application. Instead, the other Q2 statement (the natural language description in C that appears in both the versions) seems to be more complicated. The definition of arithmetical mean came to our mind as a Q4 statement. Finally, my colleague changed the Q3 statement, following the researchers' suggestion. And now, the Q3 statement follows a Gaussian distribution.*

Analyzing the changes in the design of the MERLO item from the version V1 to the version V2, what immediately comes to light is the change in the task formulation (Fig. 5).

Even with minor differences in using words, the initial task formulation comes from the previous experiences in adopting MERLO items in various contexts and it appears in the first version V1 of this MERLO item that has been designed at the beginning of the Italian research experience in mathematics education. The next version V2 shows a change in the initial task formulation, due to didactical needs.

Figure 5. Changes in the task formulation from version V1 to version V2

V1 frequencies	V2 frequencies
At least two of these five statements have equivalence of meaning. 1. Mark the statements that have equivalence of meaning; 2. Write the reasons that guided you in the choice.	1. Mark the statements (two or more) that share the same mathematical meaning; 2. Write the reasons that guided you in the choice.

Although the structure remains approximately the same, we can look at some similarities and differences. Two are the requests for the solution in both of these versions:

1. a multiple-choice selection of two (or more) out of five statements that are linked in the meaning;
2. an open answer that asks to explain the reasons of the choice.

The main difference appears in point 1 and consists in the substitution of the expression "have equivalence of meaning" with "share the same mathematical meaning". The design and implementation of MERLO items into a mathematical context may make the reader think to logical and epistemological equivalence in mathematics, but this is not the aim of MERLO items where the meaning in each statement can be linked to one another in many modalities (for example, see the application of MERLO items in a field different from mathematics like architecture, in Etkind, Kenett & Shafrir, 2010). As a consequence, the Italian team of mathematics secondary school teachers and researchers decided to change the expression to avoid misleading interpretations of the task that can arise in mathematics education. In the new formulation that appears in the second version V2 of the MERLO item the focus is on the sharing of mathematical meaning, where sharing includes not only the logical and epistemological aspects, but also the social, didactical and institutional ones, according to educational needs (Kilpatrick, Hoyles & Skovsmose, 2005).

Another interesting aspect to focus on is the change of the target statement (TS) from the version V1 to the version V2 (Fig. 6).

Figure 6. Target Statement (TS) substitution from version V1 to version V2

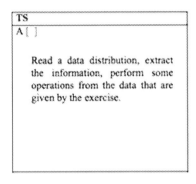
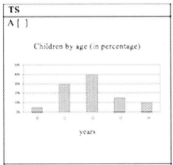

The formulation of the target statement in version V1 provides some operative instructions and looks as a task of a traditional exercise. In this case, the target statement does not communicate any mathematical meaning and it is not linked to specific frequencies distribution values.

We remind that this MERLO item is inspired by a question from INVALSI (2012). The INVALSI tests are designed as traditional tasks. Therefore, this can give a reason for the TS formulation as a traditional exercise: the teachers are more confident in such kind of task than in creating statements of MERLO items. Being at the beginning of the experience, these observations are useful to be analyzed with the Meta-Didactical Transposition in order to sketch the teachers' initial praxeology in designing MERLO items.

The task of designing MERLO items at the beginning of the experience is addressed using theoretical components of the praxologies, which are commonly already used by the teachers, recognizable within the TS formulation. These components are part of their teaching to their students, and involve: the mathematics knowledge, the pedagogical aspects and the institutional constraints.

While the experience is growing up, the teachers' initial praxeology in designing MERLO items evolve as it is reflected in the change of many statements in the MERLO item about frequencies from version V1 to version V2. The formulation of the target statement is substituted by a diagram that represents the frequencies distribution of children by age and that requires reading and interpreting the information from the graphical data distribution.

There are also some changes in the Q2 statements: while the Q2 in C remains the same from version V1 to version V2, the other Q2 in B is introduced as a new statement in the second version V2 (Fig. 7). According to the teachers' explanation, we can interpret the design choice of the Q2 in B as a simple application of the percentages that appears in the TS to a group of 200 people.

Figure 7. Q2 statements in version V2

Q2	Q2
C [ ]	B [ ]
The percentage of children who are 10 or 13 years old is the half of those who are 12 years old, and is equal to the difference between the percentage of children who are 11 years old and 14 years old.	A gym is attended by 200 children: 10 of them are 10 years old, 60 are 11 years old, 80 are 12 years old, 20 are 14 years old, and the remaining are 13 years old.

The Q2 statements in Fig. 7 are both linked to the TS in the mathematical meaning, because they share the same values of frequencies within a distribution of children with different age. According to the MERLO framework, they have the role of Q2 because they share the same mathematical meaning with the TS, but they are not similar in surface: they are represented in a natural language register, while the TS is represented in a graphical register.

Although the role of both the statements in Fig 7 is that of Q2, they require different processes to be able to recognize them as correct answers. Indeed, to be able to recognize the link between the TS and the Q2 statement in B the student as solver has to read and interpret the data distribution in a graphical register (TS) and to calculate some values of frequencies in percentage. Instead, to be able to link the TS with the Q2 statement in C the student is also required using correctly the notion of logical connectives. A notable remark comes from the face-to-face discussion, during which a teacher tries to categorize the Q2 statements in terms of difficulty: referring to the version V2, she judges the Q2 statement in B as "*a simple application*", while the Q2 statement in C "*seems to be more complicated*".

This Q2 categorization of difficulty a-priori identified by the teacher is not only her opinion and the same levels of difficulty are reflected in the experimentation with students within the classroom (Carante, 2017). This means that the teachers take into account the students' perspective, ideas, and knowledge as part of their praxeologies when designing MERLO items for their classrooms, especially in the choice of statements with a shared mathematical meaning.

For completing the analysis of the MERLO item and of the associated teachers' praxeologies when designing it, we need to consider and interpret the choice of the last two statements in D and in E. As shown in the data (the statements in Fig. 3 and 4), both in version V1 and in version V2 there are two statements, which do not share any mathematical meaning with the TS. According to the MERLO framework, they assume a different role, one of Q3 and the other of Q4, because the first one has a surface similarity with the TS and uses the same graphical register, while the second one adopts a different register of representation with respect to the TS. Focusing the attention on the Q3 statement, we can observe a change in the graph from version V1 to version V2 (Fig. 8).

Although the statement in D remains a graphical representation, which is similar with the initial one, it changes the mathematical meaning communicated to the reader. As pointed out by the teachers' face-to-face discussion (*"My colleague changed the Q3 statement, following the researchers' suggestion. And now, the Q3 statement follows a Gaussian distribution"*), the suggestion comes from the researchers who prompt the teachers to reflect on the information that they want to communicate and the effective transmitted information in the graph. In version V1, the graph seems to convey the same information as in the TS through a meaningless representation that is difficult to read and interpret. The statement in D in version V2 becomes a Gaussian distribution, which communicates some different information with respect to the TS and is similar only in appearance with it.

Analyzing the statement in E, we can observe that it deals with the arithmetic mean both in the first and in the second version of the MERLO item (Fig. 9). However, the first version calculates specific values for the mean, while the second version provides a general definition for it. The choice of changing the statement arises for avoiding any possible and ambiguous link with the TS. In the final version V2 of the MERLO item the statement in E shares neither the mathematical meaning nor the register of representation with the target statement, using a natural language definition and assuming the role of Q4.

Figure 8. Change in Q3 statement from version V1 to version V2

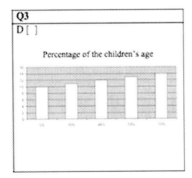
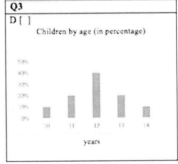

Figure 9. Changes in Q4 statement from version V1 to version V2

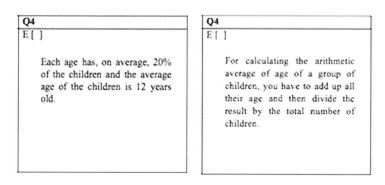

According to the Meta-Didactical Transposition framework, the shift from version V1 to version V2 highlights some changes within the Italian secondary school teachers' praxeologies in designing MERLO items. The evolution of the teachers' praxeologies happens during the experience and leads to something new and shared by the Italian team of mathematics secondary school teachers and mathematics education researchers, due to the collaboration between the two communities. For example, the new and shared formulation of the task becomes part of the praxeologies in designing MERLO items. Another remarkable observation comes from the change in the target statement from version V1 to version V2: while in a previous time the teachers try to remain consistent with the INVALSI question and with its formulation of a task, the same does not happen later in the time when they interiorize the innovative MERLO approach.

On the basis of the conducted analysis, we can outline the praxeologies in designing MERLO items that are shared between the community of teachers and the community of researchers of the Italian team. According to the idea by Chevallard (1999), we present the practical and theoretical components of the praxeologies.

The practical components are summarized into three main steps:

1. Selecting a mathematical meaning (a typical concept from the curriculum or from a question from the national assessment, like frequencies distribution) and using it to design a target statement in any register of representation (in our case a graphical register);
2. Representing the same mathematical meaning in different registers, as statements with the role of Q2 (also with many levels of difficulty, like in our case);
3. Introducing other representations with different meanings, as statements with the role of Q3 and/or Q4 (without using incorrect representations from a mathematical point of view).

Teachers Involved in Designing MERLO Items

The practical components could be justify by the theoretical components made by various theoretical frameworks and aspects:

- the MERLO framework (made by the main criteria of Meaning Equivalence and Surface Similarity);
- the epistemic nature of the mathematical contents, which are intertwined with pedagogical, didactical, and institutional aspects (national curriculum and national assessment).

In the next section we will present another research experience of designing MERLO items for the mathematics teaching, learning and assessing, carried out by an Australian team made by primary school teachers and researchers in mathematics education.

The Evolution Of The Australian Primary School Teachers' Praxeologies When Designing Merlo Items

This section shows and analyses some examples of MERLO items designed by the Australian team of primary school teachers, working in collaboration with a mathematics education researcher affiliated at the University of New England.

The data show two MERLO items in Fig. 10 and 11, which were designed by the primary teachers who also justified their design choices of their MERLO items during the designing process. Analyzing this process, we aim at outlining the Australian primary school teachers' praxeologies when designing MERLO items in mathematics education.

Figure 10. First example of MERLO item about fractions

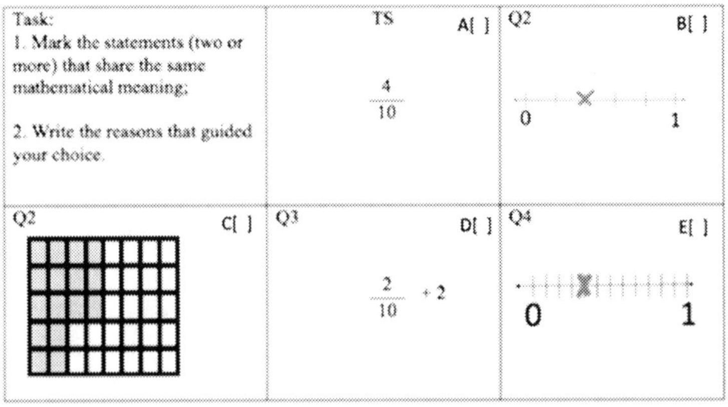

Teachers Involved in Designing MERLO Items

Figure 11. A second example of MERLO item about fractions

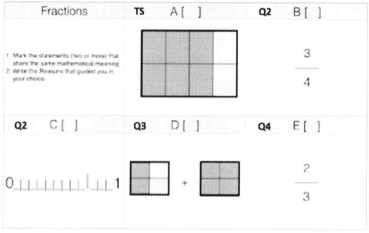

The examples are constructed around the mathematical topic of fraction that is a typical topic taught at primary schools. The topic of fractions is considered a difficult all over the world and students typically have robust misconceptions that remain over time, as pointed out by many research studies in the field (Hart, 1981, Behr et al., 1992; Stafylidou & Vosniadou, 2004).

Teachers' comments: *The target statement is four tenths. The aim of the students is to identify the statements that share the same mathematical meaning. The Q2 statements in Figure 10 are represented differently (Robutti, Arzarello, Carante, Kenett, Prodromou & Shafrir, 2016). The first Q2 statement in B represents the fraction two fifths by a linear model on a number line; the second Q2 statement in C represents the fraction sixteen fourteenths by an area model which shows the whole divided into sixteen equal parts and fourteen of them are shaded.*

The teachers' comments highlight that the starting point for designing the MERLO item is the choice of the fraction four tenths as target statement. Then, the teachers identify some other statements as Q2 that share the same mathematical meaning, but use different representations: these representations require students to identify that equivalent fractions can be represented by using different models (area, number, number line), which are commonly adopted in the classroom practices when teaching fractions. According to the teachers, the choice of different models of representations enables them to "represent the fraction as part of the whole."

In order to complete the analysis of the MERLO item and the pre-service teachers' praxeologies who designed it, we need to consider and interpret the choice of the Q3 and Q4 statements. The Q3 statement in D that has surface similarity to the TS statement (in A) but the mathematical meaning is different (Robutti et al, 2016), is represented in a numeric form like the TS. However, the value appearing in the Q3 is equal to twenty-two tenths and not to four tenths. This assesses students' understanding that the numerator and denominator are not separate values.

The Q4 statement represents four twelves on a number line and is mathematically correct but it does not share surface similarity or meaning equivalence with the target statement (Robutti et al, 2016). The Q4 statement seems to assess students understanding of the relationship between equal parts and the size of the parts, i.e. four tenths is greater than four twelfths.

Researchers' interpretation of teachers' designing of the MERLO item in figure 10 is that it seems to assess students' conceptual understanding of fractions and their knowledge about the whole-number (McNamara & Shaughnessy, 2010).

It seems that the design process of the MERLO item follows the following order: TS – Q2 – Q3 – Q4. Teachers' praxeologies evolve during that order of designing the MERLO item.

MERLO provides insights into students' thinking about fractions by posing tasks in each statement that focus on identifying students' misconceptions (Wong & Evans, 2011). A crucial aspect of MERLO assessment is the requirement to not only apply their knowledge but also explain their actions and justify their answers in order to confirm their understanding (Siegler et al., 2010). Carefully considered tasks as statements of the MERLO item accompanied with students' justifications can reveal useful information about students' thinking and strategies that can be used by teachers to plan learning experiences to consolidate correct reasoning, expand their repertoire of strategies or correct misconceptions and enhance students' reasoning.

The teacher who designed the MERLO item in Figure 11, commented that they began with constructing the MERLO item when they developed the Target Statement which represents the mathematical concept that was targeted in the learning sequence, namely to "compare fractions with related denominators and locate and represent them on a number line" (ACMNA125). Two statements with the same mathematical meaning were then developed for having a Q2 role, each with a different mathematical representation to the target statement. The teacher did not further comment on the different mathematical representations of Q2 in B and C statements. He merely mentioned that the Q3 in D statement was developed to have a similar mathematical representation to the target statement, but an alternate mathematical meaning. The Q4 in E statement was created to have both an alternate form of representation and alternate meaning to the target statement.

The MERLO was then edited to remove the Fractions, TS, Q2, Q3, and Q4 headings and replace them with headings aimed at the solver.

Teachers Involved in Designing MERLO Items

Researchers' interpretation of teachers' designing of the MERLO item in figure 11 is that it focuses on the assessment of students' knowledge and conceptual understanding of comparing fractions using statements that teachers can use to assess students' knowledge. The statements require students to identify fractions with the equal value from a variety of area models or linear models and symbolic equivalents.

The teacher/s initially constructed the target statement that shows the fraction presented by a dimensional model (area model) that shows that the whole is divided 8 equal parts and 6 of them are shaded. The TS is a "conceptual" statement that required students to apply their knowledge and explain the fraction displayed by the relative area. Students usually exhibit common errors about area models when the students focus on the number of parts instead on the equality of the parts.

Based on the TS statement, the student(s) created an equivalent Q2 statement in B, that is a numerical representation and it occurs when the number of shaded parts and the number of the whole are divided by 2. The Q2 statement in C is an equivalent representation of the TS statement on a number line. The Q3 statement in D is a graphical representation to TS with a different value that is $1+1/2$ when all the parts are added.

The teachers construct the Q4 statement in E that is a different fraction presented in a numerical form and it is required to apply procedural knowledge to employ a procedural strategy. The numerical form of the fraction in E is not equivalent to the TS statement in A but E exhibits a flawed procedural knowledge and students' misunderstandings. The Q4 Statement in E could be used by teachers to assess and rectify their students' misunderstandings.

The designing process of the MERLO assessment seemed to follow the order: TS – Q2 – Q3 – Q4.

Overall, the designing processes of designing MERLO assessments highlight a constant order of constructing the MERLO statements, starting initially with constructing the target statement and then the remaining statements Q2 – Q3 – Q4.

According to the Meta-Didactical Transposition framework, the Australian primary teachers' praxeologies follow a constant trajectory when designing MERLO items. It seemed that the teachers faithfully follow the instructions provided to them by the researcher/academic who did not only provide teachers with instructions about how they could construct each statement of the MERLO item beginning always with the TS, but she also video recorded various examples of constructing MERLO items.

The teachers were then asked to construct a MERLO item by choosing one basic concepts from the Australian curriculum. These concepts were usually taught to the primary students during year 5 or Year 6, and learned by listening to adults, following commands, participating in activities where they view the same concept expressed in different representations forms. Understanding and using different forms of basic mathematical concepts help children learn to read and understand what they've read or written in mathematical statements.

The teachers based their MERLO summative assessment on five classifications of concepts taught at year 5 or year 6. These are:

a) whole numbers and the language used when communicating the following language: ascending order, descending order, zero, ones, tens, hundreds, thousands, tens of thousands, hundreds of thousands, millions, digit, place value, expanded notation, round to, whole number, factor, highest common factor (HCF), multiple, lowest common multiple (LCM), number line, zero, positive number, negative number, integer, prime number, composite number, square number, triangular number.

b) Addition and Subtraction and the following language: plus, sum, add, addition, increase, minus, the difference between, subtract, subtraction, decrease, equals, is equal to, empty number line, strategy, digit, estimate, round to, budget.

c) Multiplication and division and the following language: multiply, multiplied by, product, multiplication, multiplication facts, area, thousands, hundreds, tens, ones, double, multiple, factor, divide, divided by, quotient, division, halve, remainder, fraction, decimal, equals, strategy, digit, estimate, round to.

d) Fractions and decimals and the following language following: whole, equal parts, half, quarter, eighth, third, sixth, twelfth, fifth, tenth, hundredth, thousandth, fraction, numerator, denominator, mixed numeral, whole number, number line, proper fraction, improper fraction, is equal to, equivalent, ascending order, descending order, simplest form, decimal, decimal point, digit, round to, decimal places, dollars, cents, best buy, percent, percentage, discount, sale price.

e) Patterns and algebra and the following language: pattern, increase, decrease, missing number, number sentence, number line, term, value, table of values, rule, position in pattern, value of term, number plane (Cartesian plane), horizontal axis (x-axis), vertical axis (y-axis), axes, quadrant, intersect, point of intersection, right angles, origin, coordinates, point, plot.

The praxeologies of the primary teachers change while teachers choose one of the five classification of concepts and its associated language. On the basis of the conducted analysis, we can outline the praxeologies when designing MERLO items that are shared between the community of primary teachers and the researcher of the Australian team. According to the idea by Chevallard (1999), the praxeologies are described below into praxis and logos.

The practical components are summarized into three main steps:

1. Choosing a mathematical concept (i.e. a fraction) as target statement and using any register to represent it (in our case a numeric and a graphical register respectively in the first example in Fig. 10 and in the second example in Fig. 11);
2. Reproducing the same mathematical concept with different graphical or numerical models (numberline, area), as statements with the role of Q2;
3. Completing the item with statements with the role of Q3 and/or Q4 (selected to assess the correct understanding of fractions).

The practical components could be justify by the theoretical components made by various theoretical frameworks and aspects:

- the MERLO framework (made by the main criteria of Meaning Equivalence and Surface Similarity);
- the epistemic nature of the mathematical contents, which are intertwined with pedagogical, didactical, and institutional aspects (national curriculum and national assessment).
- the contributions from research in mathematics education dealing with the students' difficulties in understanding fractions, intertwined with the primary school teachers' direct experience within the classrooms.

DISCUSSION

This chapter is about a joint research project, aimed at studying praxeologies of teachers involved in designing MERLO items in both Italy and Australia. The educational approach used with the teachers was not exactly the same in both countries. Differences were due to institutional constraints, in Italy, a Master for secondary teachers on mathematics education and in Australia a Master in Education for primary school teachers. Nevertheless, both educational approaches aimed at developing teachers' competences to design MERLO items autonomously. The replication of the pedagogical experiment, under these different conditions, has been useful in that it enhances the generalization of the research outcomes. For more on generalizability of findings see Kenett and Rubinstein (2018).

As first step, teachers were asked to learn about MERLO items by reading research papers, participating to lectures, solving items prepared by others. In a second step, they had to produce MERLO items on their own.

What we observed in the two experiments in Italy and Australia is that, even if the teachers come from different school levels and have worked differently on MERLO items (in Italy in groups, in Australia individually) they developed quite similar praxeologies of design, based on common institutional necessities, mathematical coherence, and didactical knowledge.

For example, Italian teachers worked on the design of items starting from questions taken by national assessment (INVALSI test for secondary level), and Australian teachers for building items took their inspiration by national curriculum.

Particularly, we can identify similarities in the process of selecting the five statements for the item, as a technique of the praxeology. The practical component can be summarized into three main steps: 1) the selection of a mathematical concept or meaning (frequencies in Italy, fractions in Australia), 2) the construction of statements sharing the same meaning with different registers of representations (numerical, graphical, verbal), and 3) the introduction of other statements that represent different concepts or meaning with respect to the previous ones (different distributions of frequencies in Italy, different values of fractions in Australia).

We also observed similarities in the theoretical counterpart of the praxeology. The two criteria of Meaning Equivalence and Surface Similarity, the mathematical and pedagogical knowledge and the institutional references appear both in Italy and in Australia as justification of the technique applied in the selection and design of the single statements. We suppose that it is possible to justify these similarities with invariants involved in designing an item: the mathematical content, the same in different countries, and the MERLO framework, also the same in both groups because it is based on the same criteria (meaning equivalence and surface similarity).

These observations suggest that MERLO items can be used in different countries by adapting them to institutional contexts, while retaining their substantial structure.

REFERENCES

Arzarello, F., Kenett, R. S., Robutti, O., Shafrir, U., Prodromou, T., & Carante, P. (2015). Teaching and assessing with new methodological tools (MERLO): a new pedagogy? In M.A. Hersh, & M. Kotecha (Eds.), *Proceedings of the First IMA International Conference on Barriers and Enablers to Learning Maths: Enhancing Learning and Teaching for All Learners*, (pp. 1-8). Glasgow, UK: Academic Press.

Arzarello, F., Robutti, O., & Carante, P. (2015). MERLO: A new tool and a new challenge in mathematics teaching and learning. In *Proceedings of the 39th Conference of the International Group for the Psychology of Mathematics Education*, (Vol. 2, pp. 57-64). Hobart, Australia: PME.

Arzarello, F., Robutti, O., Sabena, C., Cusi, A., Garuti, R., Malara, N., & Martignone, F. (2014). Meta-Didactical Transposition: A theoretical model for teacher education programmes. In A. Clark-Wilson, O. Robutti, & N. Sinclair (Eds.), *The Mathematics Teacher in the Digital Era: An International Perspective on Technology Focused Professional Development* (pp. 347–372). Dordrecht: Springer. doi:10.1007/978-94-007-4638-1_15

Behr, M. J., Harel, G., Post, T., & Lesh, R. (1992). Rational number, ratio, and proportion. In D. A. Grouws (Ed.), *Handbook of research on mathematics teaching and learning* (pp. 296–333). New York: Macmillan.

Carante, P. (2017). *MERLO items as educational tools for mathematics teachers professional development* (Unpublished Doctoral Dissertation). University of Turin, Italy.

Carante, P., & Robutti, O. (2016). *MERLO items for exploring and discussing about mathematical meanings.* Presentation 13th International Congress on Mathematical Education (ICME-13), Hamburg, Germany.

Chevallard, Y. (1999). L'analyse des pratiques enseignantes en théorie anthropologique du didactique. *Recherches en Didactique des Mathématiques, 19*(2), 221–266.

Duval, R. (2006). A cognitive analysis of problems of comprehension in a learning of mathematics. *Educational Studies in Mathematics, 61*(1-2), 103–131. doi:10.100710649-006-0400-z

Etkind, M., Kenett, R. S., & Shafrir, U. (2010). The evidence based management of learning: Diagnosis and development of conceptual thinking with meaning equivalence reusable learning objects (MERLO). *Proceedings of the 8th International Conference on Teaching Statistics.*

Etkind, M., Kenett, R. S., & Shafrir, U. (2016). *Learning in the digital age with Meaning Equivalence Reusable Learning Objects (MERLO). In Handbook of Research on Applied Learning Theory and Design in Modern Education* (Vol. 1, pp. 310–333). IGI Global.

Etkind, M., & Shafrir, U. (2011). Pedagogy for conceptual thinking: Certificate program for instructors in innovative teaching. *Proceedings of the International Conference on Education and New Learning Technologies.*

Etkind, M., & Shafrir, U. (2013). Teaching and learning in the digital age with pedagogy for conceptual thinking and peer cooperation. *Proceedings of the International Association of Technology, Education and Development Conference.*

Hart, K. (1981). Fractions. In K. Hart (Ed.), Children's understanding of mathematics: 11-16 (pp. 66-81). London: John Murray.

INVALSI. (2012). Retrieved June 30, 2016 from http://www.invalsi.it/snv2012/documenti/Ril_apprendimenti/Matematica_II_SUPERIORE_SNV2012.pdf

Kenett, R. S., & Rubinstein, A. (2018). *Generalizing research findings for enhanced reproducibility: A translational medicine case study*. Retrieved from https://papers.ssrn.com/sol3/papers.cfm?abstract_id=3035070

Kilpatrick, J., Hoyles, C., & Skovsmose, O. (Eds.). (2005). *Meaning in Mathematics Education*. New York: Springer. doi:10.1007/b104298

C. Margolinas (Ed.). (2013). Task design in mathematics education. *Proceedings of ICMI Study 22*.

McNamara, J. C., & Shaughnessy, M. M. (2010). Beyond pizzas & pies: Ten essential strategies for supporting fraction sense (Grades 3-5). Sausalito, CA: Math Solutions.

Robutti, O., Arzarello, F., Carante, P., Kenett, R., Prodromou, T., & Shafrir, U. (2016). Meaning Equivalence: a methodological tool for assessing deep understanding. *Proceedings of the International Technology, Education and Development Conference*. 10.21125/inted.2016.0735

Robutti, O., Carante, P., Prodromou, T., Arzarello, F., Kenett, R., & Shafrir, U. (in press). MERLO activities in communities of teachers and researchers: a challenge in mathematics education. In M. Isoda & L. M. Thien (Eds.), *Teacher Quality: Challenges in Mathematics Education*. Singapore: World Scientific.

Robutti, O., Cusi, A., Clark-Wilson, A., Jaworski, B., Chapman, O., Esteley, C., ... Joubert, M. (2016). ICME international survey on teachers working and learning through collaboration: June 2016. *ZDM, 48*(5), 651–690. doi:10.100711858-016-0797-5

Shafrir, U., & Kenett, R. S. (2016). *Concept science evidence-based MERLO learning analytics. In Handbook of Research on Applied Learning Theory and Design in Modern Education* (Vol. 1, pp. 334–357). IGI Global.

Siegler, R. S., Thompson, C. A., & Schneider, M. (2011). An integrated theory of whole number and fractions development. *Cognitive Development, 62*, 273–296. PMID:21569877

Stafylidou, S., & Vosniadou, S. (2004). The development of students' understanding of the numerical value of fractions. *Learning and Instruction, 14*(5), 503–518. doi:10.1016/j.learninstruc.2004.06.015

Wong, M. M., & Evans, D. (2011). Assessing students' understanding of fraction equivalence. In *Fractions: Teaching for understanding* (pp. 81–90). Adelaide, Australia: The Australian Association of Mathematics Teachers Inc.

Chapter 5
Production of Evidence-Based Informed Consent (EBIC) With Meaning Equivalence Reusable Learning Objects (MERLO):
An Application on the Clinical Setting

Myrtha Elvia Reyna Vargas
University of Toronto, Canada

Wendy Lou
University of Toronto, Canada

Ron S. Kenett
Technion Israel, Israel

ABSTRACT

Apparently, during an informed consent, patients remember little of the information given and their comprehension level is often overestimated by physicians. This study measures level of understanding of informed consent for elective cesarean surgery using an evidence-based informed consent (EBIC) model based on six MERLO assessments. MERLO recognition and production scores and follow-up interviews of 50 patients and their partners were recorded. Statistical comparison of scores within couples was performed by weighted kappa agreement, t-tests, and Ward's hierarchical clustering. Recognition score means were high for patients and partners with low standard deviation (SD), while production scores means were lower with higher SD. Clustering analysis showed that only 70% (35/50) of couples were assigned to the same cluster and t-test yields significant difference of scores within couple. Kappa yields moderate agreement levels on all items except for items D and C, which are lower. Follow-up interviews show that participants consider MERLO assessments to be helpful in improving comprehension.

DOI: 10.4018/978-1-7998-1985-1.ch005

INTRODUCTION

Data repeatedly show that patients remember little of the information disclosed during the informed consent process and that their level of comprehension is often overestimated (Hall, Prochazka, & Fink, 2012). Such issues can affect the patient and the hospital administration in many ways including health complications and repeated hospitalizations. It is therefore essential for physicians to have measurable evidence validating proper understanding of the patient on the information disclosed before signing the informed consent; however, there is a lack of tools to quantify understanding levels on the patient's side about implications, risks and possible complications of a medical intervention.

This chapter explains the application of a "Meaning Equivalence Reusable Learning Object" (MERLO) assessment designed to measure the level of comprehension of informed consent forms on elective caesarean surgery (CS). The MERLO assessments of elective CS were previously developed by Biron-Shental et al (2016) and consist of six different concepts that are part of caesarean section informed consent. This study extends the one by Biron-Shental in that it includes MERLO production tests and follow-up interviews on all participants. The goal is to explore the utility of MERLO evaluations not only to measure, but also to enhance comprehension of the knowledge domain covered by informed consent explanations. It also incorporates spouses/partners of the patients who were asked to participate in the MERLO evaluations. MERLO assessments were completed by 50 couples (patients and their partner) independently and under supervision before the patient underwent elective caesarean surgery.

The main objective of this study is the application of a MERLO tool that measures quantitatively the level of understanding of a medical informed consent, and to prove that MERLO assessments deliver evidence of high value in the clinical setting. Furthermore, resulting scores were analyzed independently and by couples with the aim of evaluating if there is statistical proof that supports shared decision making as a feasible approach for elective caesarean surgery.

Levels of understanding (measured by MERLO scores) within each couple were compared by concordance analysis using joint probability of agreement, weighted kappa agreements and hypothesis testing. A confirmatory analysis was performed using Ward's hierarchical agglomerative clustering. This study therefore provides an opportunity to investigate, not only how patients understand explanations given before signature of informed consent forms, but also the understating level of their surrounding partners.

BACKGROUND

Even though physicians may try their best to guarantee that patients have understood all necessary aspects of a medical intervention, the ability to discern the patient's actual understanding remains a complicated task. This is due to not obvious aspects involved in the process such as patient autonomy, level of stress, level of education, prior medical knowledge, etc. Previous studies have measured patient's ability to recall information provided during an informed consent process, concluding that in most cases understanding levels are lower than desired (Crepeau et al., 2011; Kiss, 2004).

The motivation of this study is the necessity to have quantitative evidence (other than a checkmark on an informed consent sheet) ensuring the physician that a patient and/or his family have understood the implications, potential risks, and alternative treatments to a medical intervention.

The procurance of discrete measures of comprehension levels could be highly beneficial to hospital administration and legal services, as it could minimize controversies and legal implications resulting from ambiguous legislation that leads to different standards and criteria for what constitutes "adequate" informed consent and that fails to clarify how far the physician should go to ensure the patient has understood every aspect of the informed consent process (Hall, Prochazka, & Fink, 2012, p. 539).

In the following sections, the definition and process of evidence-based medicine and informed consent are explained. The term "Evidence Based Informed Consent" (EBIC) is introduced as well as its purpose and importance in the gynecology and obstetrics area.

Evidence Based Medicine

Evidence based medicine (EMB) is the process of systematically finding, appraising, and using contemporaneous research findings as the basis for clinical decisions (McAlister, Graham, Karr, & Laupacis, 1999, p. 236) It relies on a uniform, conscious process of integration of individual clinical expertise with an agreed-upon interpretation of the best available, valid systematic research about what interventions have been shown to work in specific circumstances (Kapp, 2002; Sackett, 1997)

Sacket (1995) described the process of generating evidence based medicine in five general steps: i) convert patient information needs into answerable questions ii) track down the best evidence with which to answer such questions; iii) critically appraise that evidence for its validity and usefulness, iv) integrate the appraisal with clinical expertise applying the results in clinical practice, and lastly, v) evaluate one's own performance. Nowadays, additional steps towards the end of the process are suggested in the literature, for instance, physician monitoring and evaluation of any changes in the outcome is recommended so that positive effects can be supported, and negative effects remedied. Furthermore, dissemination of positive and negative results at institutional, regional, or national level is highly favored on the basis that it avoids duplication of efforts. (McAlister et al., 1999; Melnyk, Fineout-Overholt, Stillwell, & Williamson, 2010; Sackett, 1997)

In recent years, an increasing interest on EBM and a focus on the use of new methods and protocols to provide valid and updated health care information has been observed. Although mostly popular in randomized trials and meta-analysis (Kwaan & Melton, 2012), according to Rosenberg and Donald (1995) the variety of scenarios in which everyday medicine takes place allows for evidence based medicine to be practiced in any situation where there is doubt about an aspect of clinical diagnosis, prognosis, or management (Darlenski, Valentinov, Vlahov, & Tsankov, 2010; Rosenberg & Donald, 1994).

As written by Kwaan and Melton (2012), the primacy of using clinical research to guide decisions about individualized patient care originates and dominates in internal medicine and several medical subspecialties, particularly cardiology and oncology. EBM has been widely cross-applied to surgery and surgical subspecialties over the past several decades and increasing numbers of randomized controlled trials (RCTs) are performed in surgery (Kapp, 2002; Kwaan & Melton, 2012).

Nowadays, the creation and dissemination of novel procedures or clinical guidelines based on evidence that do not relate directly with a medical intervention, but rather pertain to management and administrative aspects of the clinical environment, such as the informed consent signing process, seem to be underrepresented in the literature.

Informed Consent for Clinical Treatment

According to Trougg and Joffe (2009), informed consent is the mechanism by which patients autonomously authorize medical interventions or courses of treatment (Trougg and Joffe, 2009); Hall, Prochazka and Fink (2012) state that it has become the primary paradigm for protecting the legal rights of patients and guiding the ethical practice of medicine. They also affirm that informed consent may be used for different purposes in different contexts: legal, ethical or administrative. Although these purposes overlap, they are not identical, thus leading to different standards and criteria for what constitutes "adequate" informed consent (Hall, Prochazka and Fink, 2012, p. 539).

Ideally, the informed consent process should be carried out as a conversation between a physician and a patient or family that helps them become more efficient and gives them enough information to take an autonomous decision regarding care. In their work, Biron-Shental et al (2016, p. 2) explain that current practice is based on the physician providing the patient with information that he/she deems necessary for understanding a current health issue and a proposed medical intervention. This includes alternative treatments and potential risks. Patient consent to the proposed treatment by signing the informed consent form (Biron-Shental et al., 2016). Within this context, the consent form was designed to serve only as documentation of this conversation with the aim of improving patient rights and protecting physicians. (Crepeau et al., 2011; Staples King & Moulton, 2006).

However, this process is commonly developed as an "event-based model", which can be carried at any given moment and under a variety of circumstances and diagnostic paths. Although the guiding principles indicate that it should facilitate patient autonomy in making choices, when treated as an event-based model, the process might become intricate by several well documented limitations, such as patient comprehension, patient acting under duress, patient use of disclosed information, patient autonomy, etc. In some other cases, factors beyond control of the patient such as the possibility of being compromised or not by pain, medication, disease, or social circumstance may affect the level of understanding reached or the capability to recall the information given. Other factors associated directly to the physician can also impact an informed consent outcome, such as difficulty to discern patients that experience high amounts of stress when making a clinical decision form those who easily make a decision, or lack of ability to explain information on a clear, concise and straightforward manner (i.e. without using medical jargon; see: American College of Obstetricians and Gynecologists, 2009; Anderson and Wearne, 2007; Evans, 2006).

The informed consent process can become so complex that inadvertently, the parties involved could end up carrying it out passively and as a simple signature on a form where the patient is not entirely aware of the nature, consequences and material risks of the proposed treatment (Hall et al., 2012; Moore, 2016; Recchia, Dodaro, & Braga, 2013; Staples King & Moulton, 2006).

All potential issues previously mentioned result in continuous discussions and controversies about the physician's obligations during the informed consent process to assure the patient has comprehended the information given. The guide 'Consent: A guide for Canadian physicians' written by Evans (2006), mentions that *it has been suggested that not only must the physician provide the necessary details about the nature, consequences and material risks of the proposed treatment in order to obtain informed consent, but also the physician has the duty to ensure the patient has understood the information*. Evans rejects this obligation, highlighting that such interpretation of the law would place the physician under unreasonable burden, which is understandable considering that the only tool to assess patient comprehension is their own judgement, and that it might result in difficulties for physicians to validate that the patient has a complete understanding of the procedure and its risks simply by having a conversation and a signature on a form.

The same scenario is present in relation of informed consent in obstetrics and gynecology. The American Congress of Obstetricians and Gynecologists (ACOG) emphasizes that physicians are responsible for facilitating communication, however it does not state as their responsibility to assure in depth understanding of the information related to the intervention.

The combination of factors that complicate comprehension of the informed consent under the event-based model, and failure of the current process to identify quantitatively if patients and their families are truly informed about risks, benefits, and alternatives of a medical intervention, raise doubt on the true reliability of a signed consent form.

Of course, different methods to deliver supplemental informed consent information have been implemented, such as use of audiovisuals, leaflets, webpages, etc. Even though these methods (assuming they are used by the patient) are helpful, they still do not validate the knowledge and comprehension gained by the patient with regards to a procedure.

There is a need for novel and efficient methods that improve patient comprehension and ease the evaluation of the task for physicians, allowing to assess such improvements quantitatively.

The Importance of Meaning Equivalence Reusable Learning Objects (MERLO) to Enhance Comprehension

MERLO assessments are a novel methodology for evaluating the essence of multi-dimensional, complex and conceptual situations. They are also known to enhance deep comprehension of the material reviewed. These assessments are designed to test not only the correct interpretation of the information or data provided during a teaching-learning process, but also the conceptual understanding of such information.

Etkind et al (2010) describe MERLO assessments as *a multi-dimensional database that allows the sorting and mapping of important concepts through exemplary target statements of particular conceptual situations, and relevant statements of shared meaning. Each node of MERLO is an item family, anchored by a target statement that describes a conceptual situation and encodes different features of an important concept; and also include other statements that may – or may not – share equivalence-of-meaning with the target.* (Etkind, Kenett, & Shafrir, 2010).

MERLO assessments allow quantification and data collection regarding depth of comprehension of a certain topic and provide diagnostic tools that facilitate management of the learning process by identifying certain individuals or groups with special needs and enhancing learning outcomes.

The application of MERLO assessments in the field of medicine opens new opportunities to generate evidence on learning processes that are not often evaluated and may not be as effective as expected, such as the understanding of explanations provided with informed consents. The study described in this chapter is an expanded follow up to the study in Biron-Shental et al., 2016.

Evidence Based Informed Consent (EBIC)

Evidence Based Informed Consent (EBIC) is a novel "process-based" model for obtaining a signed informed consent form. It assumes that, in addition to an informative conversation, it is also necessary to verify the depth of the patient's comprehension of the health issue and proposed medical intervention (Biron-Shental et al., 2016).

The need of Evidence Based Informed Consent arises from the fact that data repeatedly show that patients remember little of the information disclosed during the informed consent process and that their level of comprehension is often overestimated (Hall et al., 2012), in addition, research suggests that physicians may fail to meet minimal standards of disclosure for the purposes of obtaining informed consent (Campbell Philipsen, 2000).

Some studies have analyzed the level of understanding of the informed consent process in the clinical setting by conducting surveys or questionnaires with patients as participants (Crepeau et al., 2011; Hall et al., 2012; Kiss, 2004; Lashley, Talley, Lands, & Keyserligk, 2000; Tait, Voepel-Lewis, & Malviya, 2003). For instance, a survey on patients about to undergo cataract surgery and who were given informed consent found that 40% of the patients did not seek to inform themselves about the surgery prior to the consent process, and that 60% of them did not conceive cataract surgery as a risk for severe, sight threatening complications, contrary to what is explained to them during the informed consent. (Kiss, 2004). Another cohort on volunteer patients scheduled for orthopedic elective surgery completed a questionnaire to test recall of the information reviewed with their physician during the informed consent process. An average score of 70.7% correct answers was scored on the questionnaire right after the physician's explanation; this poor recall deteriorated further when patients answered the same questionnaire at a first and second post-operative visit (Crepeau et al., 2011). Some other studies have analyzed level of understanding on children or surrogates obtaining similar results. (Lashley et al., 2000; Tait et al., 2003).

To maximize the benefits of the traditional conversation process between a physician and a patient or family, an evidence based inform consent allows to measure quantitatively the level of comprehension of patients by including an assessment methodology based for conceptual thinking and deep comprehension 'Meaning Equivalence Reusable Learning Objects (MERLO)' that determines the degree of the patient's understanding of important conceptual and procedural medical issues associated with the specific health problem, as well as the proposed procedure, alternatives, and possible risks. (Biron-Shental et al., 2016). By including this two steps evaluation of understanding, EBIC is believed to increase patient motivation and engagement, encouraging the patient's direct involvement in the informed consent process and enhancing its overall comprehension.

Evidence Based Informed Consent in Gynecology and Obstetrics

The American Congress of Obstetricians and Gynecologists states that *when informed consent by the patient is impossible, a surrogate decision maker should be identified to represent the patient's wishes or best interests... (American College of Obstetricians and Gynecologists, 2009).*

Limited literature evaluating the level of comprehension of an informed consent between a patient and a surrogate exists within the gynecology and obstetrics setting. A recent qualitative study performed in the United States exploring women's decisions, perceptions, and experiences on the induction of labor process concluded, after an interview process, that women consider as reliable sources of information: clinicians, family, friends, internet, childbirth class, documentaries and popular pregnancy books (Moore, 2016).

The lack of quantitative measures of understanding between pregnant patients and their spouses (or families) during the informed consent process leave an unanswered question: how feasible is for a family member to sign an informed consent form in lieu of the patient with respect to the child labor process?

Although this is certainly a profound subject and it may result difficult to implement in a real clinical setting due to its legal implications, the EBIC methods based on MERLO assessments used in this study allow for the analysis of the previously mentioned question based on the levels of comprehension achieved by patients undergoing elective caesarean surgery, and their partners.

MATERIALS

This study is observational and includes 100 participants (50 patients and 50 spouses/partners) recruited between June 2014 - June 2015 at Mt. Sinai Hospital in Toronto, Ontario, Canada.

The study protocol, including questionnaires and interview forms, was reviewed and approved by the Mount Sinai Hospital Research Ethics Board on June 3rd, 2014.

Patient inclusion criteria for the study were:

1. Agreeing to participate in the assessment procedure.
2. Scheduled to have an elective caesarean surgery at Mt. Sinai Hospital.

All patients and their partners were consulted by their physician who explained the procedure and potential risks and complications of the intervention as part of the informed consent process either during a scheduled medical appointment or right before undergoing the intervention. All participants were then asked to fill out 6 MERLO assessment items in a supervised way, under the supervision of a physician or nurse who verified that the test was acceptably completed.

Each participant filled out the assessment alone and independently and had no communication with their partners during the exercise. This last characteristic of independence is very favorable on a study of this type as it allows participant scores to be analyzed per individual or as a couple.

After filling out 6 MERLO assessment items, subjects were interviewed regarding their informed consent experience. The assessments and interview were performed in approximately 25 minutes per subject.

Study Design

The basic concept mapping of the MERLO assessment methodology model and the conceptual topics used in this study were previously developed by Biron-Shental et al (2016) in Hebrew and were translated to English for the purpose of this study. Main differences between the two studies, in terms of the MERLO assessments, are shown in Table 1.

The study of Biron-Shentalet et al (2016) was restricted to a MERLO recognition test. MERLO assessments used in this current study consist of three parts: a recognition test, a production test, and a follow-up interview. In addition, this study incorporates results from patients and their partners. Thus, the current study extends the study in

Table 1. Data used in current study versus Biron-Shental (2016) study

	Current Study	Biron-Shental et al.
Assessment parts		
Recognition test	X	X
Production Test	X	
Follow-Up Interview	X	
Sampled subjects		
Patient	X	X
Spouse	X	

Production of Evidence-Based Informed Consent (EBIC)

Biron-Shental as it allows for more detailed results. The MERLO assessments used here consist of the following six classes of items that are considered key for the patient to understand prior to signing an informed consent for elective caesarean surgery:

1. Indications for caesarean delivery (Item A)
2. Preparation for the procedure (Item B)
3. The surgery procedure (Item C)
4. Healing process (Item D)
5. Potential complications (Item E)
6. Potential complications in future pregnancies (Item F)

All topics were presented by the physician to the patient and her accompanying partners following the general process of a common informed consent for elective caesarean surgery. Prior to the MERLO assessments, patient questions were addressed and answered, and the informed consent form was signed.

Recognition Test

Specific target statements, for each of the six topics listed above, should be fully understood by the patient prior to signing the informed consent. Based on these targets, MERLO assessment items were prepared. A detailed explanation on the developing of the six MERLO recognition assessments is given by Biron-Shental et al. (2016).

Each MERLO item is focused on one subordinate concept and includes one of the target statements. Each MERLO item includes, in addition to the target statement, four additional statements. These additional statements may be equivalent in meaning to the target statement, (i.e. a different formulation of the target statement carrying the same meaning); or may look similar to the target statement but carry a different meaning (i.e., a different formulation reusing the terms in the target statement, looking similar but having a different meaning).

All subjects were told that each MERLO item contains at least two statements with meaning equivalence, as shown in Figure 1. The general idea is that participants should mark all statements that they identify as having the same meaning as what the physician previously explained during their informed consent conversation. Assessments were graded from zero to five (5 being the highest) with a recognition score of 5 achieved when *only statements with meaning equivalence are ticked, and statements without meaning equivalence were not ticked.*

Figure 1. MERLO item of type A12

STUDY ID:		**DATE:**

A12

	[ ] 1	[ ] 2
At least two of these five statements have equivalent meaning. However, it is possible that more that two statements have equivalent meaning. 1 Mark all - *but only* - those statements that have equivalent meaning. 2 In the space below describe briefly the reasons you had in mind for making these decisions.	Elective cesarean section- a Cesarean section planned and scheduled in advance. A cesarean section is preformed whenever vaginal birth is not possible but desirable due to different reasons. It is preformed around gestational age of 39 weeks.	6 hours before the operation you must fast and avoid food and drinks. Upon admission blood samples will be obtained and fluids will be administered through an intravenous access which will be obtained according to the physician's request. Your vital signs will be recorded. External fetal monitoring will record fetal heart rate and uterine contractions.
[ ] 3	[ ] 4	[ ] 5
An Elective cesarean section is preformed around the gestational age of 39 weeks. It is preformed whenever vaginal birth is not possible or not desirable due to different reasons.	Elective cesarean section- a cesarean section planned and scheduled in advance. A cesarean section is preformed whenever vaginal birth is not possible or not desirable due to different reasons. It is preformed around the gestational age of 39 weeks.	Whenever vaginal birth is not possible or not desirable an elective cesarean section is planned and scheduled in advance, usually around gestational age of 39 weeks.

Production Test

In addition to filling out the multiple-choice sheets, patients were asked to write for each of the six MERLO items a short description of the reasons they had in mind for making these decisions (see Figure 1). These written descriptions were assessed by the physician or nurse in charge at the time of the exercise. In some instances, just a few words were written, or the writing was not considered long enough to provide a grade, in such cases the nurse or physician would request the participant to provide a more detailed explanation.

All MERLO production answers were given a score from zero to five (5 being the highest) depending on the demonstrated level of understanding by the patient. Scores from all individuals were validated by one of the co-investigators in charge of the study.

Follow-up MERLO Interviews

A brief follow-up interview was conducted with all participants. Keeping in mind that MERLO is designed as a tool to measure level of understanding rather than to enhance learning, these interviews helped researchers understand what people generally thought about the usefulness of MERLO tests and provide an insight on adequate ways of facilitating knowledge about informed consent. These interviews are meant to measure the "additional benefits" of using MERLO assessments after the informed consent, which are in theory improving and enhancing the comprehension of the information given to the patient.

The following questions were used in the interviews, as well as a note of additional comments when needed:

- On a scale of 1 to 10, how difficult was the recognition test?
- On a scale of 1 to 10, how difficult was the production test?
- After taking this survey, do you have a better understanding of elective caesarean section, and what to expect?
- Would you recommend that other women who are deciding on elective caesarean section – like you – also take such a survey?
- Would it be helpful if, during the past few weeks before taking this survey, you had an opportunity to have internet access to documents that describe in simple language different issues of elective caesarean section? For example: complications in future pregnancies.

The first two questions ranged from 1 to 10 while the last three questions were recorded with a binary yes/no answer for all respondents.

METHODS

In this study, independent levels of understanding of all participants were analyzed by descriptive statistics, however, the focus relies on analyzing similarities on MERLO scores within couples (between patient and partner). Kappa agreement, statistical hypothesis testing and hierarchical clustering analysis were used to analyze similarities on the data.

Part of the statistical analysis required treating scores as a continuous variable rather than ordinal, in such cases the scores across the six MERLO items for each participant were aggregated.

All statistical analysis was performed in R software, version 3.4.3.

Analysis on Aggregated Data

A global analysis was performed on the data; it consisted on aggregating scores of all items by individual and calculating their average score. By aggregating scores, one can treat the values as a quantitative measure rather than categorical.

A paired student t-test was used to analyze if the mean score of patients versus that of their partners was statistically significant for both recognition and production scores. The difference of the two paired scores was plotted against their mean in a Bland-Altman plot (Bland and Altman, 1995). This type of plot shows the mean score within participant pairs (patient-spouse) on the x-axis and the difference of scores within pairs in the y-axis. Blant-Altman plots include confidence limits that are helpful to visualize if there are some couples with an unusual difference in scores compared to the rest; in such case, the observation would lie outside the limit of agreement included on the plot at ± 2 standard deviations from the mean difference. Blant-Altman plots are also useful to understand if paired scores are concentrated on the higher, lower or middle part of the distribution, or if they are evenly distributed. No evident pattern observed on the observations is a good indicator that difference in scores is similarly distributed at all levels. For more on Bland-Altman plots see Franck and Govaerts (2016).

The general idea behind analyzing aggregated data with t-test and Blant-Altman plots is that if the scores were similar within each couple, the difference of their means would not be significative.

Hierarchical Clustering

Since a student t-test only shows if the two groups (patients and partners) are similar or not, it is not sufficient to understand if most couple's scores coincide, and if so, in which direction (i.e. having only high scores, only low scores, or mixed). Therefore, scores on recognition and production tests (12 scores per individual) were also examined by clustering analysis using Ward hierarchical agglomerative clustering.

Clustering analysis and machine learning are useful and powerful methods when the field of interest lacks a gold standard or cut off value that defines what is "good" and "bad" or "high" and "low". The main objective of cluster analysis is to place observations into groups (clusters) so that each cluster contains n number of observations that are more similar between them than the ones contained in the other clusters. Ideally the clusters are similar within them, and different between them.

Since the application of MERLO tests on the informed consent process is not well known yet, no gold standard is defined to differentiate high understanding from low understanding of concepts. Furthermore, clustering analysis is an adequate method to confirm (or disprove) the results obtained from the paired t-tests performed without the need of converting the data to a continuous measurement.

Walesiak and Dudek (2010, p. 1) state that the steps to perform cluster analysis are as follows:

Step 1:   Selection of variables to include
Step 2:   Selection of distance measurement/dissimilarity matrix

Step 3: Selection of clustering method
Step 4: Determining number of clusters

When analyzing continuous data, the distance measurement is most commonly Euclidean distance or some variation of it. Euclidean distance is simply calculated as the difference between two values:

$$d_{ijk} = \sqrt{\sum_{i=1}^{n}(x_i - x_j)^2}$$

.Although this distance measure can be applied to any clustering method, the results would lack useful interpretation (Walesiak & Dudek, 2010) because its calculation is designed for interval data. In fact, the main challenge for this study is that all scores are of ordinal nature; hence there is an underlying order that must be respected, and the difference between a score of 1 and 2 should not have the same effect as a difference between scores of 4 and 5. To account for this effect, Gower's generalized coefficient of dissimilarity obtained as a weighted sum of dissimilarities for each variable was used (Gower, 2012):

$$d_{ijk} = \frac{\sum_{k=1}^{n} w_{ijk} d_{ijk}}{\sum_{k=1}^{n} w_{ijk}}$$

.Where d_{ijk} represents the distance between the ith and j^{th} unit for the variable k calculated as:

$$d_{ijk} = 1 - \frac{|x_i - x_j|}{R_k}$$

.With R_k being the range of possible values of k (the ordinal variables), which in this case is 5.

Previous simulation studies on ordinal data have shown that among hierarchical clustering methods, Ward hierarchical clustering with Gower dissimilarity matrices perform best, hence that method was used to generate clusters on this study (Ferenc, 2014; Podani, 1999).

Using Ward hierarchical agglomerative clustering with Gower dissimilarity matrix on R 3.4.3 software and the "hclust" package, participants were located into 3 different clusters depending on their recognition and production results: those with high scores, those with low scores, and those with a mix of high and low scores. Scores were not aggregated prior to clustering procedure, they were rather mixed into one big pool containing patient and partner scores and afterwards, if each couple was contained within the same assigned cluster, then a proportion of similarity on scores by couple could be calculated without aggregating all scores.

In addition, clustering by Ward method was performed using dissimilarity matrices calculated from Spearman correlation and Kendall correlation. Clustering was also performed on the data by non-hierarchical approaches such as K-means and a model-based method called Latent Class Analysis. Clusters using all methods were very similar, hence the most known Ward D2 method was chosen.

Concordance Analysis on Stratified Data

Analysis on stratified data refer to scores on each MERLO item (items A to F) evaluated separately as an ordinal variable. Production and recognition scores were also evaluated separately.

Since each element of the proposed EBIC model evaluates a different aspect of the surgical procedure and following the logic that some concepts affect only the patient (i.e. general description of procedure, anesthesia, possible complications), while others require the partner's active involvement (i.e. recovery, complications of future pregnancies), some items may be of most interest to the patient alone, the partner alone, or both. A comparison of the aggregated scores may not show important features that can be observed by individual analysis, thus agreement by item is necessary. The general idea behind measuring agreement is that the greater the level of agreement between scores, the greater the feasibility of the spouse being able to consent in lieu of the patient.

Due to the different process in which production and recognition scores are calculated, different statistical analysis was applied for these two score types.

Concordance Analysis on Production Scores

It is important to remember that production scores are obtained by a physician or a nurse evaluation of each participant writing and are completely independent from recognition scores.

These scores were treated as the original rank measure they represent (0 to 5). By building a 6x6 concordance matrix for each MERLO item with the six possible scores on each axis as shown on table 2. The joint probability of agreement (P_o) was calculated as the proportion of observations falling within the main diagonal of the agreement matrix; that is, the proportion of patients and partners that obtained the same scores.

Since there are 6 items conforming the MERLO assessment, six concordance matrices as the one shown in table 2 were obtained.

Concordance Analysis on Recognition Scores.

Recognition scores also follow an ordinal fashion, but unlike production tests, recognition tests allow respondents to simply guess or check boxes randomly when uncertain of the right answers. The joint probability calculation used with production scores fails to take into consideration the possibility of guessing correctly merely by chance. A more robust method, the Cohen Kappa coefficient of agreement accounts for this chance agreement (Heo, 2008; Tang et al., 2015). This method

Production of Evidence-Based Informed Consent (EBIC)

Table 2. Concordance matrix of production scores on MERLO item A. Main diagonal shown in gray

		Partner Score					
		0	1	2	3	4	5
Patient Score	0	0	-	-	-	-	-
	1	-	0.02	-	-	-	-
	2	-	-	0.10	0.04	-	-
	3	-	0.02	0.04	0.04	0.10	-
	4	-	-	0.02	0.08	0.06	0.06
	5	-	0.02	0.02	0.06	0.08	0.24

improves upon the joint probability of agreement in that it incorporates the values outside the main diagonal into the calculation. All kappa coefficients of agreement were calculated using the "kappa2" package in R 3.4.3 software. (Matthias, Lemon, Fellows, & Puspendra, 2015).

As in the previous example posed when clustering, these scores continue to be of ordinal nature. For instance, a couple of patient-partner with scores of 5 and 4 ought not have the same impact on agreement level as a patient-partner with scores of 2 and 1; even though the difference between both cases is just 1, there must be more weight or more "impact" placed on a couple of participants that scored lower.

To account for the importance in difference between scores, Fleiss-Cohen weights were calculated:

$$w_{ij} = 1 - \frac{(c_i - c_j)^2}{(c_i - c_r)^2}$$

Where c_i and c_j are patient and partner scores and c_r is the maximum score of 5 that can be obtained in the recognition test (Tang et al., 2015).

Weights in the diagonal cells (perfect agreement) are equal to 1 and decreasing weights (up to zero) are generated as the values get farther from the diagonal. The weights matrix calculated is shown in table 3.

The Fleiss Cohen weights previously calculated (w_{ij}) are incorporated into the joint probability matrix by multiplying them by the proportion of agreement for each couple. A weighted Cohen Kappa coefficient was computed for each recognition MERLO item using the following Cohen Kappa formula:

$$K_w = \frac{\sum_{i=1}^{k}\sum_{j=1}^{k} w_{ij} P_{ij} - \sum_{i=1}^{k}\sum_{j=1}^{k} w_{ij} P_{i+} P_{+j}}{1 - \sum_{i=1}^{k}\sum_{j=1}^{k} w_{ij} P_{i+} P_{+j}}$$

Table 3. Fleiss-Cohen weights matrix calculated for recognition scores. Main diagonal shown in gray

		\multicolumn{6}{c}{Partner Score}
		0	1	2	3	4	5
Patient Score	0	1	0.96	0.84	0.64	0.36	0
	1		1	0.96	0.84	0.64	0.36
	2			1	0.96	0.84	0.64
	3				1	0.96	0.84
	4					1	0.96
	5						1

Cohen Kappa coefficients are always less than or equal to 1 with a value of 1 implying perfect agreement.

As indicated by Lantz and Nebenzahl (1995) the levels of Kappa agreement can be affected by the configurations of the data in the agreement matrix. As shown in figure 2, highest kappa values are obtained when a symmetrical (balanced) distribution of scores in the agreement categories is observed, regardless of a complete symmetric distribution of disagreement categories (Figure 2, center) or a complete skewing (Figure 2, right) of disagreement categories; in other words, if the main diagonal has a high agreement and the upper part of the matrix has very low agreement compared to the lower part, or vice versa. By contrast, the minimum value of Kappa is obtained by maximally skewing agreement into a single agreement category and having disagreement categories symmetrically distributed (Figure 2, left) (Lantz and Nebenzahl, 1996).

Figure 2. Different distributions of agreement. 1) Skewness of agreement and balance of disagreement categories. 2) Balance on agreement and disagreement categories. 3) Balance of agreement and skewness on disagreement categories

1	
a	b
b	0

2	
a	b
b	a

3	
a	b
0	a

Since most participants scored high on recognition tests, recognition scores data have agreement levels highly skewed toward the upper score levels; to reduce the effects of skewness in recognition Kappa values, unbalance in disagreement categories was minimized by collapsing the lowest score categories 0,1, and 2 into a single category, and relabeled the scores from 0 to 3, thus 4x4 concordance matrices were obtained.

As a final note on the importance of measuring agreement in this study, it is worth mentioning that although similar in appearance, agreement is a fundamentally different concept from correlation and a high value on the latter does not automatically imply a good agreement. Our interest is not to measure the association of changes in patient and partner scores, but to understand if the scores are consistent between the two, that is why Kappa agreement was used as the concordance measure in this study (Tang et al., 2015).

Analysis on Follow-Up Interview

After analyzing scores of all couples and locating them in a cluster, the answers to questions 1 and 2 from follow-up interviews related to difficulty of the exercise were compared to the belonging cluster of every individual in a cross-tabulation matrix. Ideally a person with high scores on the assessments would rate the exercise as easy on the follow-up questions while a person with lower scores would find them difficult. In questions 1 and 2 of the interviews, participants were asked to provide a score from 1 to 10 depending on how difficult the MERLO recognition and production scores were. These data were reclassified in 3 levels to ease cross-tabulation with belonging clusters: level 1 corresponding to a perceived difficulty between 1 and 3, level 2 for difficulty between 4 and 6, and level 3 for difficulty of 7 or more. Descriptive statistics were calculated for questions 3, 4, and 5 of the follow-up interviews.

RESULTS

Data Summary

Scores on MERLO recognition and production tests from 50 patients and their partners at Mount Sinai Hospital in Toronto, Canada, were obtained. The mean and standard deviation on aggregated recognition scores for the group of patients was slightly higher than that of their partners, with 4.14 and 0.504 respectively, while for the group of partners was 3.98 and 0.611. Mean scores on aggregated production tests were lower, with higher standard deviations, this is expected given

Production of Evidence-Based Informed Consent (EBIC)

that participants were required to write a sentence summarizing their understanding, rather than having a multiple-choice setting. Mean on production scores was more balanced within couples but with more variation between couples, with a mean score of 3.67 and 3.37 for patient and partner respectively, while standard deviation was 0.99 and 0.95.

Figures 3 and 4 show the distribution of raw scores on each MERLO subcategory.

Roughly, better performance on all participants is observed on items A and D: Indications for caesarean Delivery and Healing process respectively. Lowest scores are present on item F of recognition (Potential complications of future pregnancies) tests and items B and E of production tests (Preparation for the procedure and Potential complications, respectively) for both patients and partners. It is also noted that patients tend to score slightly higher in recognition exercises, but in production tests, for patients who scored at or below 3, their spouses generally obtain a higher

Figure 3. Recognition scores bar plot per each MERLO subcategory

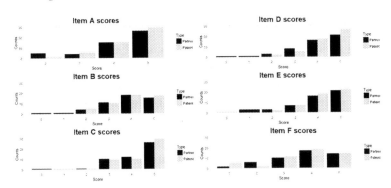

Figure 4. Production scores bar plot for each MERLO subcategory

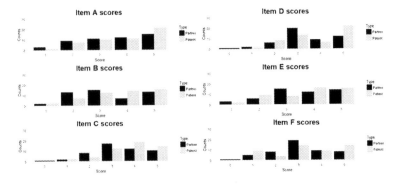

Production of Evidence-Based Informed Consent (EBIC)

score. One observation from a spouse was missing on MERLO item F on both recognition and production tests. These missing data was imputed as the average score for the remaining items of the same individual in production and recognition scores. Imputation did not affect significantly the distribution of data.

Results of Aggregated Data

Results from paired t-test on recognition scores indicate that there is no statistical difference between recognition scores of patients and partners, however the p-value obtained is at borderline (mean diff. = 0.149, p-value= 0.05). Bland-Altman plot (Figure 5) shows the same average of differences of 0.149 with the upper and lower agreement limits at -0.87 and 1.17 respectively, leaving only 2 observations outside this area and another 2 at borderline level.

With regards to production scores, results from the paired t-test indicate that the difference between scores of patient and partner is statistically significant (mean diff. = 0.316, p-value= 0.002). Bland-Altman plot (Figure 6) shows the upper and lower agreement limits at -1.02 and 1.65 respectively, 4 observations lye outside the agreement limits and 2 are located at borderline.

There is no evident pattern on the distribution of observations, which is a good indicator that difference in scores is similarly distributed at all levels.

Results of Hierarchical Cluster Analysis

Using Gower dissimilarity matrix and Ward hierarchical clustering, 3 clusters were obtained. Cluster 1 contained individuals with high scores (N=30, Mean = 4.475, SD = 1.19), cluster 2 was formed by individuals with a combination of high and low

Figure 5. Bland-Altman plot of differences between aggregated patient and partner on recognition scores. Mean of difference is the central dashed line. Agreement limits are represented by the upper and lower dashed lines. Observation ties are represented by red lines

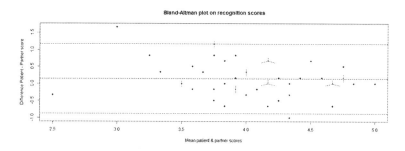

Production of Evidence-Based Informed Consent (EBIC)

Figure 6. Bland-Altman plot of differences between aggregated patient and partner on production scores. Mean of difference is the central dashed line. Agreement limits are represented by the upper and lower dashed lines. Observation ties are represented by red lines

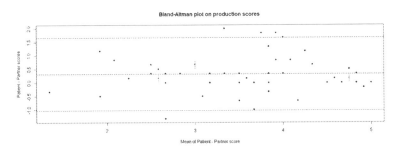

scores (N = 35, Mean = 3.85, SD = 1.18) and cluster 3 contained participants with mostly low scores (N = 35, Mean = 3.15, SD = 1.19). The clusters had overlapping of subjects which can be observed in figure 7, with some of them laying only on cluster 1 or cluster 3. In the same figure can be observed how cluster 2 contains individuals with a mixture of high and low scores.

Figure 7. Resulting clusters from Ward hierarchical clustering using Gower's dissimilarity matrix

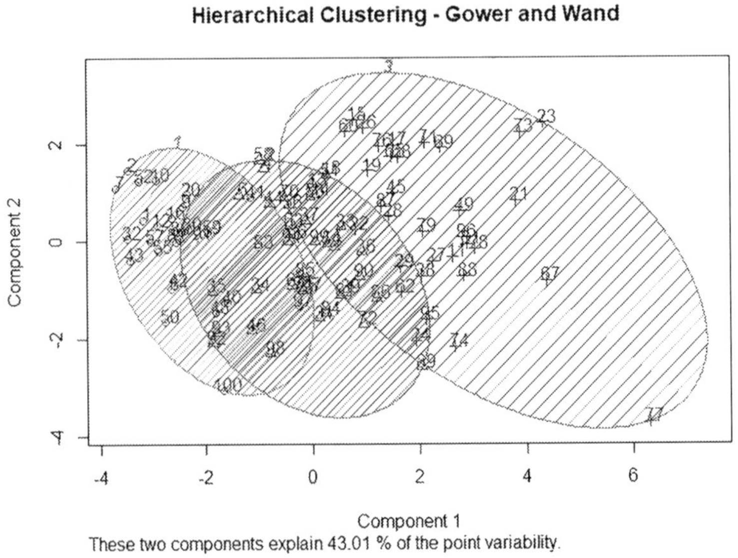

Production of Evidence-Based Informed Consent (EBIC)

The principal components identified for clustering were items D and E of the production test which pertain to healing process and possible complications, respectively. This means that scores from these two items had most weight when assigning individuals to a cluster. This makes sense because recognition scores were very homogeneous (most participants had high scores) in comparison to production scores, thus clustering was mainly driven by the latter. The predominance of production scores for clustering can be observed in figure 8 where the cluster groups get closer and, in some instances overlap to the right of the black dashed line that separates production form recognition results.

By clustering analysis, one can differentiate individuals scoring higher from those that obtained lower scores. Table 4 below shows the obtained distribution in individual counts for each category. 35 individuals were classified in cluster 2, having a mix of high and low scores either on production or recognition tests. Individuals classified as cluster 2 are located in either of the two grey fields of Table 4.

Once the three clusters were defined, whether a couple was part of the same cluster or not was analyzed to conclude on similarity of scores within couples. 70% of the pairs tested (35/50) were found within the same cluster.

Results of Agreement Analysis

As expected from the bar plots shown in Figure 3, the joint probability of agreement for item A is generally higher for scores of 5, but due to a relatively high number of partners scoring 2 with respect to patients, agreement is also high at scores of 2. The joint probability of agreement and the Cohen-Kappa coefficient of agreement

Figure 8. Mean scores per cluster at each MERLO item. Each line represents a cluster

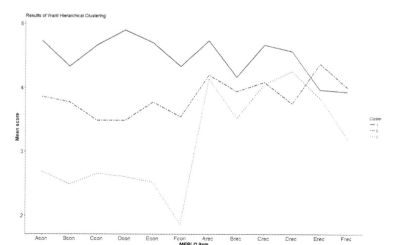

Production of Evidence-Based Informed Consent (EBIC)

Table 4. Counts of individuals within cluster 1 (high scores) and cluster 3 (low scores)

	Recognition Score			
	High	Low		
Cluster 1: n = 30	-	High	Production Score
-	Cluster 3: n = 35	Low	

for each item are shown in Table 5. The joint probability of agreement is also shown graphically on heat maps in Figure 9 and 10. The main diagonal represents the cases in which patient and partner obtained the same scores (perfect concordance). Cohen suggested the Kappa result be interpreted as follows: values ≤ 0 as indicating no agreement and 0.01–0.20 as none to slight, 0.21–0.40 as fair, 0.41–0.60 as moderate, 0.61–0.80 as substantial, and 0.81–1.00 as almost perfect agreement.

Since all Kappa values obtained in recognition and production tests range from 0.4 to 0.6 (except for item D on recognition testing with Kappa=0.344), and following Cohen interpretation, the general agreement of comprehension level is moderate for all items, and it's fair for item D.

It is important to point out the paradox that causes kappa scores to increase by unbalanced disagreement, rather than making them decrease (refer to Figure 2). From the heat maps one can see that even though the perfect agreement categories on recognition scores are more apparent compared to the production scores heat maps, recognition kappa values are lower. This is due to the high unbalanced agreement present in production scores, which, in combination with good agreement in the main diagonal, yields higher Kappa values.

Table 5. Joint probability of agreement, Cohen-Kappa coefficient of agreement and Cohen Kappa p-value of recognition scores for each MERLO item

MERLO item	Recognition scores			Production Scores		
	Joint probability	Cohen-Kappa	p-value	Joint probability	Cohen-Kappa	p-value
A	0.7	0.406	0.002	0.46	0.571	0.00002
B	0.64	0.521	0.0001	0.46	0.344	0.0112
C	0.66	0.426	0.002	0.50	0.555	0.00002
D	0.56	0.419	0.0008	0.50	0.468	0.0004
E	0.66	0.444	0.001	0.60	0.641	0.000005
F	0.58	0.529	0.0001	0.52	0.597	0.00001

Production of Evidence-Based Informed Consent (EBIC)

Figure 9. Heat maps of agreement between patient-partner production scores by MERLO item

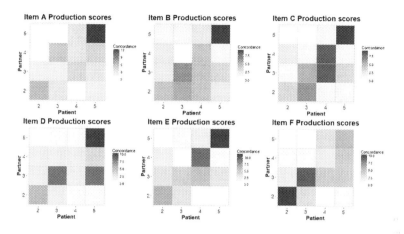

Figure 10. Heat maps of agreement between patient-partner recognition scores by MERLO item

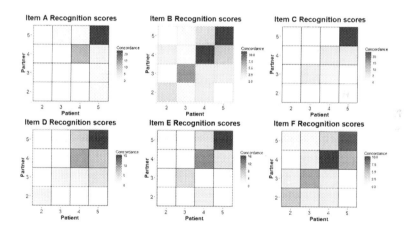

Such unbalance was accounted for in production scores by merging the lowest scores into one category; that approach was not effective on recognition scores because the unbalance is present at all score levels rather than in the lowest end.

Weighted Cohen Kappa coefficients for recognition tests were also calculated after dichotomizing original scores into: 0-3 = low scores and 4-5 = high scores. As shown in table 6, in all cases Cohen-Kappa values decreased slightly, most probably due to the increase in unbalance on agreement categories.

Table 6. Cohen-Kappa coefficient of agreement and Cohen Kappa p-value after dichotomization of recognition scores for each MERLO item

MERLO item	Cohen-Kappa (binary)	p-value (binary)
A	0.30	.029
B	0.541	0.0001
C	0.492	0.0005
D	0.389	0.003
E	0.607	.00001
F	0.614	0.00001

Results of Follow-Up Interviews

Follow-up interviews allow researchers to understand if MERLO assessments can be extended as a mean to enhance understanding of the informed consent process. Results from cross-tabulation between assigned clusters and reclassified difficulty levels from questions 1 (related to recognition test difficulty) and 2 (related to production test difficulty) are shown in Table 7.

Table 7. Cross-tabulation of assigned clusters and perceived difficulty of MERLO recognition (top) and production (bottom) tests

	Recognition Test			
	Perceived Test Difficulty			
Assigned Cluster	1 - Easy	2 - Medium	3 - Hard	Total
1 - High Score	25	5	-	30
2 - High & Low	23	8	4	35
3 - Low scores	18	14	3	35
Total	66	27	7	100

	Production Test			
	Perceived Test Difficulty			
Assigned Cluster	1 - Easy	2 - Medium	3 - Hard	Total
1 - High Scores	11	13	6	30
2 - High & Low	8	15	12	35
3 - Low Scores	13	12	10	35
Total	32	40	28	100

Production of Evidence-Based Informed Consent (EBIC)

Most individuals classified recognition tests as an easy task, still 27% of those were in the cluster of low score recipients. Those that thought the test was of medium difficulty were mostly located in the same cluster of lower scores. No individual with only high scores (cluster 1) considered the test as a hard task.

Difficulty of scores on production tests are more evenly distributed compared to recognition tests. This is a direct indicative that writing exercises are more difficult for users. 71% of the participants who obtained overall low scores (cluster 3) considered the exercise of low or medium difficulty, this could indicate that they thought they performed better on the writing exercise. There is a small group of subjects (N = 6) that considered the exercise as difficult but still were classified as high scores (cluster 1). It is important to remember that the clustering analysis was mainly driven by production scores, thus the cross-tabulation of recognition scores should be interpreted carefully.

Based on answers to question 3, 4, and 5, 89.5% of the patients considered that they had a better understanding of elective caesarean section after the exercise; 93.7% would recommend that other woman perform the test; and 98% thought they would benefit with having internet access to material that describe in simple language issues involved with caesarean section; their partners had very similar opinions, with 89.6%, 91.6%, and 98% agreeing to questions 3, 4 and 5 (mentioned above) respectively; these data is visually described in figure 11.

Figure 11. Results of questions 2, 3, and 4 of follow-up interview

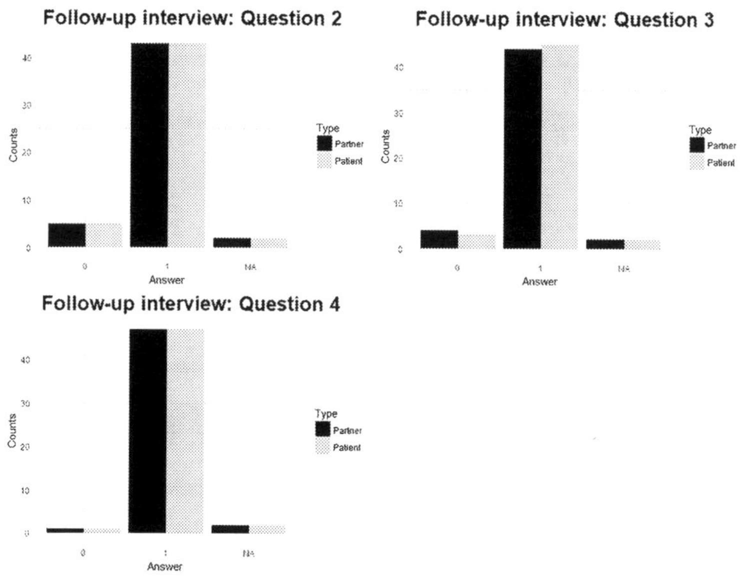

Two couples failed to answer questions 2, 3, and 4 from the post MERLO interviews due to unknown reasons.

CONCLUSION

This is the first study of this type that incorporates production exercises to validate and interpret recognition scores, in addition to post-interviews that corroborate the use of MERLO assessments in the clinical setting as a tool to enhance comprehension.

The study proves that MERLO assessments are a valuable tool in the clinical setting, as they offer physicians a discrete measure of patient's level of understanding of an informed consent that may minimize the issues and controversies commonly generated by this process. In addition, the application of this tools benefits patients as well, by engaging them in the informed consent process and enhancing deep comprehension of the information provided.

The inconsistent results obtained by t-test on aggregated data and hierarchical agglomerative Ward clustering indicate that using a surrogate in the complete informed consent is not a justified/good approach for elective caesarean surgery. Still, results from concordance analysis by separate items (not - aggregated data) using Kappa agreements show that a surrogate could oversee signing informed consent for *some* of the concepts involved (while some items are understood better by the patient, others are surprisingly comprehended better by their partner); this may serve as an indication of the areas of the informed consent in which the presence of a spouse or family member may be more beneficial to the patient.

Even though this study incorporates a bigger sample size and more elaborated MERLO assessments, there are aspects that, if included in further studies, could help better understand the role of individual characteristics in the comprehension of informed consents (i.e. age group, socio-economical status, education level, etc.).

In conclusion, the application of MERLO assessments to obtain Evidence Based Informed Consent is a novel procedure whose implementation should be explored further, as it provides several significant advantages: it benefits the patient in many ways; protects physicians of burdens related to ensuring patients understanding of important aspects of a medical intervention; and it provides valuable data that can be used to improve the informed consent process.

ACKNOWLEDGMENT

The authors would like to acknowledge Uri Shafrir for his help with this paper.

REFERENCES

American College of Obstetricians and Gynecologists. (2009). *Informed Consent*. Retrieved from https://www.acog.org/Clinical-Guidance-and-Publications/Committee-Opinions/Committee-on-Ethics/Informed-Consent

Anderson, O. A., & Wearne, M. J. (2007). Informed consent for elective surgery—what is best practice? *Journal of the Royal Society of Medicine, 100*(1), 97–100. doi:10.1258/jrsm.100.2.97 PMID:17277283

Biron-Shental, T., Kenett, R., Shafrir, U., Rosen, H., Garg, S., Farine, D., & Fishman, A. (2016). Evidence Based Informed Consent for Caesarean Section Using MERLO - Meaning Equivalence Reusable Learning Objects. *British Journal of Education, Society & Behavioral Science, 17*(2), 1–10. doi:10.9734/BJESBS/2016/27163

Campbell Philipsen, N. (2000). In the Patient's Best Interest: Informed Consent or Protection from the Truth? *Journal of Perinatal Education, 9*(3), 44–47. doi:10.1624/105812400X87789 PMID:17273218

Crepeau, A. E., Mckinney, B. I., Fox-Ryvicker, M., Castelli, J., Penna, J., & Wang, E. D. (2011). Prospective Evaluation of Patient Comprehension of Informed Consent. *The Journal of Bone and Joint Surgery, 93*(19), 1–7. doi:10.2106/JBJS.J.01325 PMID:22005875

Darlenski, R. B., Valentinov, N., Vlahov, V. D., & Tsankov, N. K. (2010). Evidence-based medicine : Facts and controversies. *Clinics in Dermatology, 28*(5), 553–557. doi:10.1016/j.clindermatol.2010.03.015 PMID:20797518

Etkind, M., Kenett, R. S., & Shafrir, U. (2010). The evidence-based management of learning: diagnosis and development of conceptual thinking with meaning equivalence reusable learning objects (MERLO). In *International Conference on the Teaching of Statistics ICOTS-8* (pp. 1–19). Retrieved from http://iase-web.org/documents/papers/icots8/ICOTS8_1C3_ETKIND.pdf

Evans, K. G. (2006). *Consent: A guide for Canadian physicians* (4th ed.). Retrieved February 3, 2018, from https://www.cmpa-acpm.ca/en/advice-publications/handbooks/consent-a-guide-for-canadian-physicians

Ferenc, R. (2014). Clustering Methods for Ordinal Variables. *Economic Questions, Issues and Problems*, 274–279.

Gower, J. C. (2012). A General Coefficient of Similarity and Some of Its Properties. *Biometrics, 27*(4), 857–871. doi:10.2307/2528823

Hall, D. E., Prochazka, A. V., & Fink, A. S. (2012). Informed consent for clinical treatment. *Canadian Medical Association Journal, 184*(5), 533–540.

Heo, M. (2008). Utility of Weights for Weighted Kappa as a Measure of Interrater Agreement on Ordinal Scale. *Journal of Modern Applied Statistical Methods, 7*(1), 205–222. doi:10.22237/jmasm/1209615360

Kapp, M. B. (2002). Evidence-based Medicine and Informed Consent. *Academic Medicine, 77*(12), 1199–1200. doi:10.1097/00001888-200212000-00007 PMID:12480621

Kiss, C. G. (2004). Informed Consent and Decision Making by Cataract Patients. *Archives of Ophthalmology, 122*(1), 94. doi:10.1001/archopht.122.1.94 PMID:14718302

Kwaan, M. R., & Melton, G. B. (2012). Evidence-based medicine in surgical education. *Clinics in Colon and Rectal Surgery, 25*(3), 151–155. doi:10.1055-0032-1322552 PMID:23997670

Lantz, C. A., & Nebenzahl, E. (1996). Behavior and Interpretation of the k Statistic: Resolution of the Two Paradoxes. *Journal of Clinical Epidemiology, 49*(4), 431–434. doi:10.1016/0895-4356(95)00571-4 PMID:8621993

Lashley, M., Talley, W., Lands, L. C., & Keyserligk, E. W. (2000). Informed Proxy Consent: Communication between pediatric surgeons ans surrogates about surgery. *Pediatrics, 105*(3), 591–597. doi:10.1542/peds.105.3.591 PMID:10699114

McAlister, F. A., Graham, I., Karr, G. W., & Laupacis, A. (1999). Evidence-based medicine and the practicing clinician. *Journal of General Internal Medicine, 14*(4), 236–242. doi:10.1046/j.1525-1497.1999.00323.x PMID:10203636

Melnyk, B. M., Fineout-Overholt, E., Stillwell, S. B., & Williamson, K. M. (2010). Evidence-based practice: step by step: the seven steps of evidence-based practice. *The American Journal of Nursing, 110*(1), 51–53. doi:10.1097/01.NAJ.0000366056.06605.d2 PMID:20032669

Moore, J. E. (2016). Women's Voices in Maternity Care: The Triad of Shared Decision Making, Informed Consent, and Evidence-Based Practices. *The Journal of Perinatal & Neonatal Nursing, 30*(3), 218–223. doi:10.1097/JPN.0000000000000182 PMID:27465453

Podani, J. (1999). Extending Gower's General Coefficient of Similarity to Ordinal Characters. *International Association for Plant Taxonomy, 48*(2), 331–340. doi:10.2307/1224438

Recchia, V., Dodaro, A., & Braga, L. (2013). Event-based versus process-based informed consent to address scientific evidence and uncertainties in ionising medical imaging. *Insights Into Imaging, 4*(5), 647–653. doi:10.100713244-013-0272-6 PMID:23904249

Rosenberg, W., & Donald, A. (1994). Evidence based medicine : An approach to clinical problem-solving. *BMJ (Clinical Research Ed.), 310*(6987), 1122–1126. doi:10.1136/bmj.310.6987.1122 PMID:7742682

Sackett, D. L. (1997). Evidence-Based Medicine. *Seminars in Perinatology, 21*(1), 3–5. doi:10.1016/S0146-0005(97)80013-4 PMID:9190027

Staples King, J., & Moulton, B. W. (2006). Rethinking informed consent: The case for shared medical decision making. *American Journal of Law & Medicine, 32*(4), 429–501. doi:10.1177/009885880603200401 PMID:17240730

Tait, A. R., Voepel-Lewis, T., & Malviya, S. (2003). Do They Understand? (Part II). *Anesthesiology, 98*(3), 609–614. doi:10.1097/00000542-200303000-00006 PMID:12606902

Tang, W., Hu, J., Zhang, H., Wu, P., & He, H. (2015). Kappa coefficient : A popular measure of rater agreement. *Shanghai Jingshen Yixue, 27*(1), 62–67. PMID:25852260

Trougg, R. D., & Joffe, S. (2009). *Consent to Medical Care: The Importance of Fiduciary Context*. doi:10.1093/acprof

Walesiak, M., & Dudek, A. (2010). Finding groups in ordinal data: An examination of some clustering procedures. *Studies in Classification, Data Analysis, and Knowledge Organization*, 185–192. doi:10.1007/978-3-642-10745-0-19

KEY TERMS AND DEFINITIONS

Concordance: Level of agreement between two variables. It measures whether scores are consistent between them (as one increases the other increases in the same amount, or vice versa).

Correlation: Statistical measure of how strongly two pairs of continuous variables are related. Within a clinical context, correlation is useful when the two variables being tested represent different clinical or physiologic parameters usually measured in different units.

Evidence-Based Informed Consent (EBIC): Process-based model for obtaining a signed informed consent form. It assumes that, in addition to an informative conversation, it is also necessary to verify the depth of the patient's comprehension of the health issue and proposed medical intervention to follow.

Hierarchical Clustering: Data driven statistical method used to place observations into groups (clusters) with a predetermined ordering from top to bottom. Each cluster contains "n" number of observations that are more similar between them than the ones contained in the other clusters.

Kappa Statistic: Statistical method frequently used to test interrater reliability between two categorical variables. It accounts for the possibility that raters or survey respondents actually guess on at least some variables due to uncertainty.

Meaning Equivalence Reusable Learning Objects (MERLO): Multi-dimensional database that allows the sorting and mapping of important concepts through exemplary target statements of conceptual situations, and relevant statements of shared meaning.

Ordinal Data: A categorical data type for which the values have naturally ordered categories and the distance between such categories is unknown. An example of ordinal measure is the Likert scale.

Chapter 6

Using Concept Maps With Errors to Identify Misconceptions:
The Role of Instructional Design to Create Large-Scale On-Line Solutions

Paulo Rogério Miranda Correia
https://orcid.org/0000-0003-2419-7103
University of São Paulo, Brazil

Joana Aguiar
University of São Paulo, Brazil

Brian Moon
Perigean Technologies, USA

ABSTRACT

Concept maps (Cmaps) have been successfully used to make knowledge structures visible. During Cmap task elaboration, novice students are likely to suffer cognitive overload, and they might avoid coping with difficult contents staying in his semantic safe territory. The authors have developed an innovative approach using Cmaps with embedded errors applied on Sero! – a cloud-based knowledge assessment platform. This chapter presents a case study involving the current use of Cmaps with errors as an assessment task capable of identifying misconceptions about the advances of molecular biology. Undergraduate students (n=86) were asked to find the errors hidden into the propositional network. The results confirmed the task challenged the students to go beyond their safe semantic territory. Misconceptions were readily identified from the students' answers providing good insights for the development of a bespoke feedback. The current data available is enough to foresee a broad range of research opportunities to readers interested in concept mapping, instruction and learning analytics.

DOI: 10.4018/978-1-7998-1985-1.ch006

INTRODUCTION

Knowledge representation is a crucial part of developing conceptual understanding. This process requires selecting and organizing relevant pieces of information retrieved from the long-term memory to create an external depiction of our mental models. Concept maps (Cmaps) have been successfully used to this aim as they can make our knowledge structures visible (Hay, Kinchin & Lygo-Baker, 2008; Novak, 2010). Cmaps are an organized set of propositions (*e.g.*, initial concept – linking phrase → final concept) that reveal the meaning of conceptual relationships. The inclusion of linking phrases to clarify conceptual relationships makes Cmaps more suitable than other graphical organizers used to represent knowledge and information accurately (Authors, 2012; Davies, 2011). The examples below illustrate how the propositional meaning can be drastically changed with discrete modifications in the linking phrases. They represent different ways to express the conceptual relationship between 'propositions' and 'meaning.'

- **Propositions – ???? → meaning:** the linking phrase is missing.
  - There is only an association between the concepts 'meaning' and 'proposition', but nothing is revealed about the nature of their relationship. There is no proposition in this example.
- **Propositions – and → meaning:** the linking phrase does not present a verb.
  - The use of 'and' creates one single concept 'proposition and meaning', which does not carry any meaning. There is no proposition in this example.
- **Propositions – contain → meaning:** the linking phrase presents only a verb.
  - The verb is related to the initial concept, and a coherent message is conveyed. There is a proposition in this example, allowing us to evaluate the correctness of its content (in this case, it is correct). The verb is an essential element of the linking phrase.
- **Propositions – must contain → meaning:** the linking phrase presents more than a verb.
  - The linking phrase can contain other elements to improve content accuracy. This example is more accurate than the last one.
- **Propositions – do not contain → meaning:** the linking phrase presents a verb.
  - One word (not) can invert the meaning of the message. Therefore, it is necessary to wisely select the words when writing the propositions to ensure that they represent our ideas. This example presents a proposition once the message is understandable, but its content is not conceptually correct.

The semantic content present in Cmaps is valuable to reveal how the conceptual relationships are organized into our mental models. For this reason, concept mapping has been reported in the literature for organizing, sharing, and preserving knowledge (*e.g.*, Authors, 2012; Kinchin, 2014; Novak, 2010; Authors, 2011).

The Mapper Needs to Know How to Create Cmaps

Meaning negotiation is straightforward when good Cmaps are produced. Training novice users is critical to avoid cognitive overload (Sweller, Ayres & Kalyuga, 2011). During the Cmap elaboration, the mapper must handle simultaneously the task format (create a good Cmap with clear propositions) and the content to be mapped (a topic under study). One way to reduce the cognitive load imposed during the Cmap elaboration can be observed when the student decides not to deal with the most challenging content, staying in his/her semantic safe territories. However, not only misconceptions and conceptual mistakes might be kept hidden but also the discussions about them were unlikely to be aroused during the meaning negotiation. The potential use of Cmaps to foster deep learning cannot be verified under these circumstances (Authors, 2017).

Experts acting as mappers are a possible alternative that deserves to be explored from the instructional design point of view (Authors, 2016; Authors, in press). There are many variables to adjust to create Cmap-based tasks for large-scale purposes using technology. The authors have developed an approach for using Cmaps with embedded errors prepared by the expert and delivered online through Sero!, a cloud-based knowledge assessment platform (Authors, 2017). In this task, students are asked to find the errors hidden into the propositional network (no visual cues are provided). As a consequence, students must go beyond their safe semantic territory exploring problematic knowledge and threshold concepts added by the teacher/expert. Misconceptions and conceptual mistakes are readily identified from the students' answers, and individual feedback can be prepared and delivered considering the content that needs to be intensely studied.

This chapter describes a case study involving the current use of Cmaps with errors as an assessment task capable of identifying misconceptions. Next part details the research context and the procedures adopted for the empirical data collection and analysis. The results highlight the difficulty level of the errors added to the Cmap and the evaluation of the students' performance on the task. A comparison among propositions which explicitly declares the equivalence between the concepts ($A - is\ equivalent\ to \rightarrow B$) highlights the potential that simple statements have to include errors in the Cmap. Assessment tasks based on Cmap with errors are in the early stages of development, and future research directions are pointed out at the end of the chapter.

MISCONCEPTIONS ABOUT MOLECULAR BIOLOGY ADVANCES: A CASE STUDY

Research Context

Eighty-eight undergraduate students enrolled in the Natural Science Course offered at the University of São Paulo (Brazil) took part in this study. The data collection occurred during the formal assessment scheduled to check students' conceptual understanding about the advances in molecular biology. The flipped-classroom approach (Reidsema, Kavanagh & Hadgraft, 2017) was chosen to allow more interaction with the students, considering they have to be prepared for the following discussions in the classroom. Additionally, the teacher can adjust the emphasis on the topics according to the specific interests (or difficulties) of different groups of students. The flipped-classroom approach fosters an engaging learning environment when it is carefully planned, which is crucial to encourage students to choose deep rather than surface learning. The main contents were addressed throughout a 5-class sequence, summarized below (each class lasts 105 min).

- **Evolutionism:** Class #1
    - Creationism and evolutionism: two different ways to explain the complexity of life.
    - The intelligent design concept.
    - Principles of Natural Selection Theory.
    - Earth's age and the scientific evidence that supports evolution.
- **Molecular Biology:** Class #2
    - Review of concepts regarding molecular biology, such as DNA translation, the human genome and mutations.
    - Advances in molecular biology related to cloning and stem cells.
- **Ethical issues and scientific research:** Class #3
    - Ethical issues on scientific researches involving health issues.
- **Ethical issues and society:** Class #4
    - The concept of bioethics and the implications of molecular biology advances in contemporary society.
- **Assessment:** Class #5
    - Formal assessment using the Cmap with errors task.

Data Collection Using the Cmap with Errors

Figure 1 shows the Cmap about the topics to be evaluated containing 26 concepts and 32 propositions to address the focus question, *"How can molecular biology*

Figure 1. Cmap with errors (highlighted in grey boxes) developed for assessing students' understanding of molecular biology advances. Focal question: How can molecular biology affect human life?

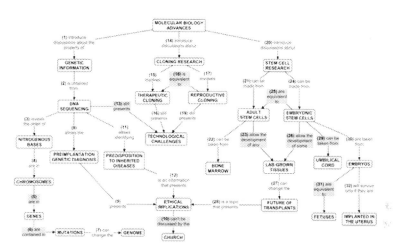

affect the lives of humans?". Modifications in 10 linking phrases were made to include conceptual errors at propositions 5, 6, 10, 13, 18, 23, 25, 26, 29 and 31. These errors were categorized into non-scientific or scientific according to the content expressed by the proposition (Table 1). Additionally, secondary categories were used to differentiate the scientific propositions into:

- **Biochemistry (BC):** conceptual relationships about the molecular biology of the cells.
  - Example: Genes – are contained in → mutations (P6)
- **Stem cells (ST):** conceptual relationships to differentiate embryonic and adult stem cells.
  - Example: Embryonic stem cells – can be taken from → umbilical cord (P29)
- **Explicit equivalence (EE):** conceptual relationships comparing two similar concepts.
  - Example: Reproductive cloning – is equivalent to → therapeutic cloning (P18)

Other categories can be selected if the subject or the teacher's interests are different.

The Cmap with errors was distributed to the students using Sero! (https://www.serolearn.com/), a learning assessment software platform that uses concept mapping to assess knowledge and learning (Figure 2). Goals for Sero! include overcoming the

Table 1. *Scientific and non-scientific errors added to the Cmap. Scientific errors were further categorized as biochemistry (BC), stem cell (SC) and explicit equivalence (EE).*

ID	Proposition	Non-Scientific	Scientific	Secondary categories
P5	Chromosomes – are in → genes		X	BC
P6	Genes – are contained in → mutations		X	BC
P10	Ethical implications – can't be discussed by the → Church	X		-
P13	DNA sequencing – still presents → technological challenges	X		-
P18	Reproductive cloning – is equivalent to → therapeutic cloning		X	EE
P23	Adult stem cells – allow the development of any → lab-grown tissues		X	SC
P25	Embryonic stem cells – are equivalent to → adult stem cells		X	EE
P26	Embryonic stem cells – allow the development of some → lab-grown tissues		X	SC
P29	Embryonic stem cells – can be taken from → umbilical cord		X	SC
P31	Embryos – are equivalent to → fetuses		X	EE

challenges of implementation and supporting adaptive learning by helping teachers and instructional system designers get a more in-depth insight into learner progression, particularly in the advancement of higher-order thinking skills (Moon et al., 2018).

Analysis of the Students' Outcomes

Errors' Level of Difficulty

The total of students who identified each error was calculated to classify the errors into easy (identification rate ≥ 60%), moderate (60% < identification ≥ 40%) and difficult (identification < 40%). These percentages were chosen considering the assessment task was applied after the study period (classes 1-4), and students who grasp the content are capable of identifying the added errors. Descriptive statistics parameters were calculated to compare students' performance on identifying scientific and non-scientific errors.

Figure 2. Cmap with errors delivered to the students using Sero!.

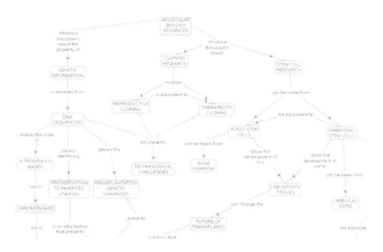

Students' Performances

Individual marks were calculated as follows: students received 1 point for each identified error (max. 10 points). A histogram was plotted to represent the students' overall performance. Additionally, a matrix S (88x10) was elaborated considering each student in the line (88 students) and each error in the column (10 errors). If the student found the error he received 1 point and if the students have not found the error he received 0 points. Using this matrix, a hierarchical cluster analysis was carried out with Euclidian distance and Ward/Incremental iteration method in Pirouette 4.5. The aim was to look for natural groups of students with similar response patterns.

RESULTS AND DISCUSSION

The Level of Difficulty of the Errors Added to the Cmap

Figure 3 shows the percentage of students who identified each added error. The overall students' performance was 42%, and they were slightly better dealing with the non-scientific (average: 51%; median: 51%) than the scientific errors (average: 40%; median: 37%). However, the most identified error (75.0%) involved the relationship between embryos and fetuses (P31, *embryos – are equivalent to → fetuses*), which is a content related to general embryology. The differences in these developmental stages are enormous, and they must be acknowledged to avoid misunderstandings

Figure 3. Students' performance on finding the errors added to the Cmap (EE: explicit equivalence; SC: stem cells; BC: biochemistry)

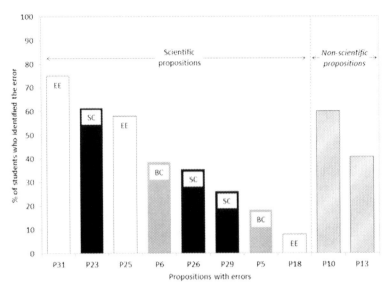

about embryonic stem cells (*e.g.*, Sadler, 2012). The broad media coverage has contributed to disseminate this scientific topic, but the oversimplification and distortion may generate some confusion to people unfamiliar with the technical jargon (Jurberg et al., 2009). It is worthy to note the lack of conceptual clarity may affect the judgment about this controversial issue that involves an explicit ethical dimension (Stewart, Dickerson & Hotchkiss, 2009). The concepts 'embryo' and 'fetuses' were presented and contrasted during class 2 to highlight the impact of this misunderstanding on judging stem cell research. We discussed the frozen embryos produced at fertility clinics and the final destination they receive when the donors are not interested in having more children. The claim that discharged embryos may be useful to the advance of the research using embryonic stem cells was chosen to clarify the difference between embryos and fetuses. The effectiveness of the classroom discussions may explain the high percentage of students who found this error in the Cmap. The task revealed two other easy errors involving stem cells (61.4%; P23: *adult stem cells – allow the development of any → lab-grown tissues*) and a non-scientific proposition (60.2%; P10: *ethical implications – can't be discussed by the → Church*). The former confirmed that the majority of students recognized limitations for the use of adult stem cells to produce tissues in a laboratory, and the latter shed light into societal institutions beyond science which are interested in the discussion about molecular biology advances.

Using Concept Maps With Errors to Identify Misconceptions

Two errors classified in the moderate level of difficulty were in P25 (58.0%; *embryonic stem cells – are equivalent to → adult stem cells*) and P13 (40.9%; *DNA sequencing – still presents → technological challenges*). Despite the identification rate difference being minimal, P23 (61.4%) and P25 (58.0%) were classified as easy and moderate errors, respectively. It is worth to highlight the identification rates were arbitrarily defined, following our previous experience with a Cmap with errors about climate change (Authors, in press). However, they can be changed to reflect the specificities of each application providing reliable information for both teacher and students. P23 and P25 have the same content (stem cell), and their identification rates confirmed they presented the same level of difficulty. Figure 4a uses circles to show the number of students, who did not find these errors, found only one of them and found both errors. The circle sizes at the end of axes confirm these errors presented a similar level of difficulty. Moreover, the big circle at the upper right quadrant highlights that P23 and P25 were quickly identified.

The error in P13 (*DNA sequencing – still presents → technological challenges*) was about some technical challenges for sequencing DNA, which was compared to the obstacles that need to be overcome for cloning (see P16: *therapeutic cloning – still presents → technological challenges* and P19: *reproductive cloning – still presents → technological challenges*). To evaluate these errors, the students needed to recall that therapeutic and reproductive cloning are not routinely procedures because scientific advances are not mature yet. This comparison (see P13, P16 and P19 in Figure 1) involving the concept of "technological challenges" makes P13 a subtle error in contrast to P10 (*ethical implications – can't be discussed by*

Figure 4. Comparison of the identification rates for (a) P23 x P25 (similar difficulty level) and (b) P23 x P26 (different difficulty levels). The sizes of the grey circles indicate the relative amount of students who did not find any error (lower left corner), found only one (end of axes) and found both errors (upper right corner).

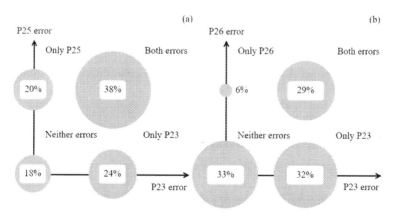

the → Church). Despite being non-scientific errors, because they did not consider conceptual relationships between biochemistry and molecular biology, P13 (40.9%) presented a lower identification rate than P10 (60.2%).

The concept of 'lab-grown tissues' presented an inversion when we consider both P23 (61.4%; *adult stem cells – allow the development of any → lab-grown tissues*) and P26 (35.2%; *embryonic stem cells – allow the development of any → lab-grown tissues*). The embryonic stem cells are more versatile than the adult ones, explaining why these propositions were wrong. The levels of difficulty, in this case, were not similar (Figure 4b). Surprisingly, the P26 error was found by fewer students than P23 and, therefore, the proposed comparison was not accomplished by most of them. This valuable information about these specific conceptual relationships is readily available for the teacher, who can plan activities to remediate this problem. Maybe, a discussion highlighting P23 and P26 together would be helpful to contrast the differences between embryonic and adult stem cells.

Errors presented in P5 (18.2%; *chromosomes – are in → genes*) and P6 (36.4%; *genes – are contained in → mutations*) explored the microscopic nature of the molecular biology. These biochemical propositions challenged students to check the hierarchy of the concepts 'chromosomes', 'genes' and 'mutations.' The identification of these errors required the understanding of genes, which are within chromosomes and can present mutations. The inversion of the directional arrow (see P5 and P6 in Figure 1) in both cases generated two subtle errors, involving scientific contents. These aspects explain why P5 and P6 were difficult to find. However, the most challenging error in this Cmap was in P18 (8.0%; *reproductive cloning – is equivalent to → therapeutic cloning*). Despite being explored during classes 3 and 4, the ethical differences between reproductive and therapeutic cloning were not enough to draw students' attention. We hypothesize that the similarities involving the cloning technical procedures discussed in class 2 were preferentially recalled, explaining why 92.0% of students did not find this error. This value is untypically high even for difficult errors. There is a need to further investigation about what kind of meaning the students have about the propositions considering all the content discussed throughout classes 1-4. Our case study did not take this kind of data into account, opening a broad space for future studies on qualitative issues (*e.g.*, Are difficult errors due to the content? Are there issues related to the way the proposition was written?).

Evaluation of the Students' Performances

Figure 5 shows the overall students' performance on the Cmap with error assessment task. The average mark was 4.2 (SD=1.9) considering the 0-10 scale. The histogram confirmed the assessment task captured the different level of understanding achieved

Figure 5. Overall students' performance on the Cmap with error assessment task.

by the students during the study period (classes 1-4). It is worth mentioning that 72.7% (n=64) of the students' marks ranged from 2.1 to 6.0. Nineteen students (21.6%) showed marks above 7.1, and 8 students (5.7%) presented an inferior performance (marks below 2.0). Students with scores below 4.0 (38.6%; n=34) deserve detailed feedback from the teacher to get appropriate instructions about how to deal with the found learning obstacles. The Cmap with error task was applied after the study period, and higher marks were expected.

All students' answers were taken into account to run the hierarchical cluster analysis. Five natural groups (G1-G5) were identified, and the main features are presented in Table 2. The groups were ordered according to the level of performance on the assessment task. G1 contains the students (n=22) with the highest average performance on scientific (62%) and non-scientific content (66%). Their main failures were in the low identification rate for P3 (22.7%) and P18 (0.0%). G2 (n=11) can be considered as the classroom average when we observe their performance on scientific (49%) and non-scientific content (46%), while P5 (9.1%), P18 (0.0%), P26 (18.2%) and P29 (18.2%) were propositions especially difficult to them. It is worth mentioning these students found the error P23 easier than P26, which is the pattern showed in Figure 4b. G3 has a distinguishable feature in comparison to all other groups. Some of these students (n=23) found the error in P18 (30.4%), which is the most difficult one in this assessment (only 8.0% of the students found it, see Figure 3). On the other hand, they had problems to find the errors in P6 (4.3%), P13 (13.0%), P23 (30.4%), P26 (21.7%) and P29 (4.3%). G4 gather students (n=21) with difficulties to find several errors added to the Cmap (see P5, P6, P13,

P18, P25, P26, and P29 in Table 2). The average performance was low (scientific: 28%; non-scientific: 62%), and these students need to be aware of the importance of reviewing part of the content about the advances of molecular biology. This message must be part of the feedback provided by the teacher. Surprisingly, all G4 students found the P10 error, and they have a non-scientific average higher when compared to G1-G3 (Table 2). G5 presents the students (n=11) that had the worst performance on the assessment task. The average percentages on scientific (18%) and non-scientific (41%) were lower than the values verified for G1-G4. The high level of identification of P13 (81.8%) increased the non-scientific average to 41%, repeating the pattern observed for G4. However, these students could not find the errors at the propositions P5 (0.0%), P10 (0.0%), P18 (0.0%) and P26 (0.0%). Other errors were identified at low rates, such as P6 (9.1%), P23 (18.2%) and P25 (27.3%). Teachers' feedback is important for any student, but it is critical for the G5 ones. The need for a rapid intervention is a clear route to avoid the accumulation of conceptual problems that might hinder meaningful learning (Kinchin, Lygo-Baker & Hay, 2008; Novak, 2002).

Table 2. Groups of students found by hierarchical cluster analysis considering their performance on the task (% of students who identified the error).

Propositions with errors			G1 (n=22)	G2 (n=11)	G3 (n=23)	G4 (n=21)	G5 (n=11)
Scientific	BC	P5	22.7	9.1	30.4	14.3	0.0
	BC	P6	50.0	100.0	4.3	38.1	9.1
	ST	P23	100.0	63.6	30.4	76.2	18.2
	ST	P26	100.0	18.2	21.7	9.5	0.0
	ST	P29	54.5	18.2	4.3	14.3	45.5
	EE	P18	0.0	0.0	30.4	0.0	0.0
	EE	P25	77.3	100.0	82.6	4.8	27.3
	EE	P31	90.9	81.8	78.3	66.7	45.5
Average (SD) for scientific propositions with error		-	62(37)	49(42)	35(30)	28(29)	18(19)
Non-scientific		P10	68.2	45.5	52.2	100.0	0.0
		P13	63.6	45.5	13.0	23.8	81.8
Average (SD) for non-scientific propositions with error		-	66(3)	46(0)	33(28)	62(54)	41(58)
Overall average (SD)		-	66(33)	48(37)	35(28)	35(34)	23(28)

Explicit Equivalence as a Way to Create Errors

Among several ways to include errors in the Cmap, the explicit equivalence deserved particular attention due to its simplicity. The idea is to declare that two concepts are equivalent (*A – is equivalent to* → *B*) to verify if the students can find the error. From the expert point of view, this kind of equivalence is rarely correct as we exemplified in P18 (*reproductive cloning – is equivalent to* → *therapeutic cloning*), P25 (*embryonic stem cells – are equivalent to* → *adult stem cells*) and P31 (*embryos – are equivalent to* → *fetuses*). On the other hand, novices may not be ready to recognize differences when the concepts A and B are wisely chosen. The use of this straightforward approach was tested, and Figure 6 shows graphics to combine the identification rates for P18, P25, and P31.

The errors in P18 (*reproductive cloning – is equivalent to* → *therapeutic cloning*) is about cloning, and the main differences between reproductive and therapeutic cloning were ethical, considering the discussions made during classes 3 and 4. There are similarities involving technical procedures in both types of cloning, making this error even more subtle. The small circles we found in Figures 6a, and 6c are due to the low identification rate observed to P18, which it is much more difficult than P25 (see Figure 6a) and P31 (see Figure 6c). The classroom discussions after the assessment confirmed that the students could not differentiate between the 'technical' equivalence and the 'ethical' non-equivalence between these types of cloning. This piece of information was useful to teacher clarifies the conceptual aspects readily because the Cmap with errors made this learning obstacle visible. Accurate and timely feedback is critical to foster pedagogic resonance, *i.e.*, the bridge between teacher knowledge and student learning (Kinchin, Lygo-Baker & Hay, 2008; Trigwell & Shale, 2004).

Figure 6b confirms P25 and P31 are easier than P18 (lowest percentage for 'neither errors'), and P31 (*embryos – are equivalent to* → *fetuses*) is easier than P25 (*embryonic stem cells – are equivalent to* → *adult stem cells*). Both propositions are about general embryology, but the conceptual difference between embryos and fetuses are much easier to grasp. The conceptual richness to differentiate what are the differences between embryonic and adult stem cells asks for a broad repertoire in this topic. For example, the understanding of stem cells is necessary to promote its progressive differentiation using new qualities and attributes (*e.g.*, the ability to develop lab-grown tissues), which can also be included into the Cmap with errors (see P23 and P26 in Figure 1). To sum up, explicit equivalence is a valid format to create propositions with errors without masking the contents' level of difficulty. This feature is critical if the teacher wants to probe the course's semantic territory

Using Concept Maps With Errors to Identify Misconceptions

to find problematic knowledge and hidden threshold concepts (Meyer & Land, 2005). Explicit equivalence should be combined with other ways to include errors

Figure 6. Explicit equivalence to include errors in the Cmap using P18 (difficult), P25 (moderate) and P31 (easy). The combining effects of P18 x P25, P25 x P31, and P31 x P18 are presented in (a), (b), and (c), respectively.

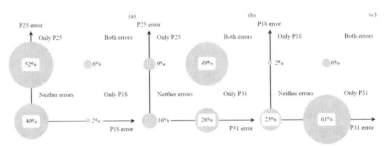

Figure 7.

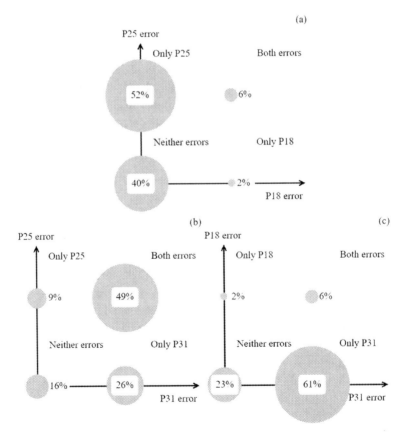

as we did in Figure 1 (*e.g.*, inversion in the reading direction as in P5-P6, initial concept inversions as in P23-P26, and use of negatives as in P29) ensuring enough information to identify and characterize students' misconceptions.

FUTURE RESEARCH DIRECTIONS

Cmap with errors is a straightforward approach to identify students' misconceptions. The current data available is enough to foresee a broad range of research opportunities to readers interested in concept mapping, instruction and learning analytics.

- **Task Format:** Students can be asked to identify errors and make comments to justify them. Bloom's taxonomy shows that finding errors is simpler than explaining why a conceptual relationship is wrong (Krathwohl, 2002). Peers can discuss the comments through collaborative activity in the classroom or online platforms.
- **Error Format:** New ways to include errors in the Cmap should be explored. The case study presented in this chapter is just a starting point with a few examples that can be expanded. Even straightforward solutions such as explicit equivalence can produce lots of valuable information. The challenge is to find out appropriate formats to create subtle errors to distinguish students with different levels of understanding.
- **Epistemological Inputs:** Different academic disciplines present diverse knowledge structures. The kind of conceptual relationships can also vary due to epistemological differences we find between scientific, humanities, and social science courses (Donald, 1983). The overall Cmap structure may reflect these differences and the Cmap-with-error assessment task should be tested in other knowledge areas beyond molecular biology and climate change (Authors, in press).
- **Concept Selection:** The expert has the opportunity to map the semantic territory of the content to be taught and search for hidden threshold concepts (Meyer & Land, 2005). They may be seen as learning obstacles by the students, and the feedback makes a difference to scaffold them to struggle the understanding portals the experts already crossed. Future research can show how to include threshold concepts and problematic knowledge into Cmap with error assessment task.
- **Feedback Effect:** An accurate, timely and bespoke feedback can be provided to the students considering the errors found. The format of this feedback and its impact regarding learning outcomes promise research avenues. The Cmap

with error assessment task is amenable to online platforms, and learning analytics can be used to report the information about the student and the group misconceptions (Clow, 2013).

REFERENCES

Clow, D. (2013). An overview of learning analytics. *Teaching in Higher Education, 18*(6), 683–695. doi:10.1080/13562517.2013.827653

Davies, M. (2011). Mind mapping, concept mapping, argument mapping: What are the differences and do they matter? *Higher Education, 62*(3), 279–301. doi:10.100710734-010-9387-6

Donald, J. G. (1983). Knowledge structures – methods for exploring course content. *The Journal of Higher Education, 54*(1), 31–41.

Hay, D., Kinchin, I. M., & Lygo-Baker, S. (2008). Making learning visible: The role of concept mapping in higher education. *Studies in Higher Education, 33*(3), 295–311. doi:10.1080/03075070802049251

Jurberg, C., Verjovsky, M., Machado, G. O. C., & Affonso-Mitidieri, O. R. (2009). Embryonic stem cell: A climax in the reign of the Brazilian media. *Public Understanding of Science (Bristol, England), 18*(6), 719–729. doi:10.1177/0963662509335457

Kinchin, I. M. (2014). Concept Mapping as a Learning Tool in Higher Education: A Critical Analysis of Recent Reviews. *The Journal of Continuing Higher Education, 62*(1), 39–49. doi:10.1080/07377363.2014.872011

Kinchin, I. M., Lygo-Baker, S., & Hay, D. B. (2008). Universities as centres of non-learning.*StudiesinHigherEducation,33*(1),89–103.doi:10.1080/03075070701794858

Krathwohl, D. R. (2002). A Revision of Bloom's Taxonomy: An Overview. *Theory into Practice, 41*(4), 212–218. doi:10.120715430421tip4104_2

Meyer, J. H. F., & Land, R. (2005). Threshold concepts and troublesome knowledge (2): Epistemological considerations and a conceptual framework for teaching and learning. *Higher Education, 49*(3), 373–388. doi:10.100710734-004-6779-5

Moon, B., Johnston, C., & Moon, S. (2018). A Case for the Superiority of Concept Mapping-Based Assessments for Assessing Mental Models. *Proc. of the Eighth Int. Conference on Concept Mapping*. Medellín, Colombia.

Novak, J. D. (2002). Meaningful learning: The essential factor for conceptual change in limited or inappropriate propositional hierarchies leading to empowerment of learners. *Science Education, 86*(4), 548–571. doi:10.1002ce.10032

Novak, J. D. (2010). *Learning, creating, and using knowledge: concept maps as facilitative tools in schools and corporations.* New York, NY: Routledge. doi:10.4324/9780203862001

Reidsema, C., Kavanagh, L., & Hadgraft, R. (2017). *The flipped classroom: practice and practices in Higher Education.* Singapore: Springer. doi:10.1007/978-981-10-3413-8

Sadler, T. W. (2012). *Langman's medical embryology.* Baltimore, MD: Lippincott Williams & Wilkins.

Stewart, C. O., Dickerson, D. L., & Hotchkiss, R. (2009). Beliefs About Science and News Frames in Audience Evaluations of Embryonic and Adult Stem Cell Research. *Science Communication, 30*(4), 42752. doi:10.1177/1075547008326931

Sweller, J., Ayres, P., & Kalyuga, S. (2011). *Cognitive load theory.* New York, NY: Springer. doi:10.1007/978-1-4419-8126-4

Trigwell, K., & Shale, S. (2004). Student learning and the scholarship of university teaching. *Studies in Higher Education, 29*(4), 523–536. doi:10.1080/0307507042000236407

ADDITIONAL READING

Anderson, L. W. (2013). *A Taxonomy for Learning, Teaching, and Assessing: A Revision of Bloom's Taxonomy of Educational Objectives.* New York, NY: Pearson Higher Education.

Ifenthaler, D., & Hanewald, R. (2014). *Digital Knowledge Maps in Education: Technology-Enhanced Suppport for Teachers and Learners.* New York, NY: Springer. doi:10.1007/978-1-4614-3178-7

Kinchin, I. M. (2016). *Visualising powerful knowledge to develop the expert student.* Rotterdam: Sense Publishers. doi:10.1007/978-94-6300-627-9

Larusson, J. A., & White, B. (2014). *Learning analytics: from research to practice.* New York, NY: Springer.

Meyer, J. H. F., & Land, R. (2006). *Overcoming Barriers to Student Understanding.* New York, NY: Routledge. doi:10.4324/9780203966273

Meyer, J. H. F., Land, R., & Baillie, C. (2010). *Threshold Concepts and Transformational Learning.* Rotterdam: Sense Publishers.

Salmon, D., & Kelly, M. (2015). *Using Concept Mapping to Foster Adaptive Expertise: Enhancing Teacher Metacognitive Learning to Improve Student Academic Performance.* New York, NY: Peter Lang Publishing. doi:10.3726/978-1-4539-1436-6

Torres, P. L., & Marriott, R. C. V. (2010). *Handbook of Research on Collaborative Learning Using Concept Mapping.* Hershey, PA: IGI Global. doi:10.4018/978-1-59904-992-2

Related Readings

To continue IGI Global's long-standing tradition of advancing innovation through emerging research, please find below a compiled list of recommended IGI Global book chapters and journal articles in the areas of culturally responsive pedagogy, professional development, and education preparation. These related readings will provide additional information and guidance to further enrich your knowledge and assist you with your own research.

Adams, M. G. (2018). Systematically Investigating Instructor Impact on Student Satisfaction in Graduate Programs. In D. Polly, M. Putman, T. Petty, & A. Good (Eds.), *Innovative Practices in Teacher Preparation and Graduate-Level Teacher Education Programs* (pp. 200–214). Hershey, PA: IGI Global. doi:10.4018/978-1-5225-3068-8.ch012

Adeyele, V., & Aladejana, F. (2019). Comparative Effectiveness of Interactive Multimedia, Simulation Games, and Blended Learning on Science Performance of Learners With Special Needs. In J. Keengwe (Ed.), *Handbook of Research on Blended Learning Pedagogies and Professional Development in Higher Education* (pp. 340–356). Hershey, PA: IGI Global. doi:10.4018/978-1-5225-5557-5.ch019

Adjei-Boateng, E., & Cobbinah, J. E. (2019). Secondary School Teacher Preparation in the Age of Inclusive Education. In B. Rice (Ed.), *Global Perspectives on Inclusive Teacher Education* (pp. 30–42). Hershey, PA: IGI Global. doi:10.4018/978-1-5225-7703-4.ch003

Akyüz, A., Tanış, A., Khalil, E., Ardıç, Ö., & Mede, E. (2018). Integrating Culture in Language Classrooms: The Effects in Teaching and Learning. In D. Polly, M. Putman, T. Petty, & A. Good (Eds.), *Innovative Practices in Teacher Preparation and Graduate-Level Teacher Education Programs* (pp. 579–602). Hershey, PA: IGI Global. doi:10.4018/978-1-5225-3068-8.ch030

Amzat, I. H., & Li, C. A. (2019). The State of Education and Employment of People With Visual Impairment in Malaysia. In B. Rice (Ed.), *Global Perspectives on Inclusive Teacher Education* (pp. 137–155). Hershey, PA: IGI Global. doi:10.4018/978-1-5225-7703-4.ch009

Anohah, E., & Suhonen, J. (2018). Conceptual Model of Generic Learning Design to Teach Cultural Artifacts in Computing Education: An Analysis Based on Akan Culture in Ghana. *International Journal of Online Pedagogy and Course Design*, 8(4), 50–64. doi:10.4018/IJOPCD.2018100104

Araujo, R. C., & Gadanidis, G. (2018). Online Discussion Tools in Teacher Education: Threaded Forums and Collaborative Mind Maps in a Mathematics Education Program. In D. Polly, M. Putman, T. Petty, & A. Good (Eds.), *Innovative Practices in Teacher Preparation and Graduate-Level Teacher Education Programs* (pp. 530–556). Hershey, PA: IGI Global. doi:10.4018/978-1-5225-3068-8.ch028

Bai, H. (2018). Preparing Teacher Education Students to Use Instructional Technology in an Asynchronous Blended Course. In D. Polly, M. Putman, T. Petty, & A. Good (Eds.), *Innovative Practices in Teacher Preparation and Graduate-Level Teacher Education Programs* (pp. 603–619). Hershey, PA: IGI Global. doi:10.4018/978-1-5225-3068-8.ch031

Baker, L. L., Liu, L. B., & Milman, N. B. (2016). International Conceptualizations of Diversity in Multi-Cultural Teacher Preparation: A Review of the Literature 2006-2015. *International Journal of Information Communication Technologies and Human Development*, 8(3), 16–33. doi:10.4018/IJICTHD.2016070102

Boboc, M. (2018). Redesigned Urban Teacher Preparation: A Reflective, Community-Centered, Clinically Intensive Program at a Midwestern Public Research University. In D. Polly, M. Putman, T. Petty, & A. Good (Eds.), *Innovative Practices in Teacher Preparation and Graduate-Level Teacher Education Programs* (pp. 327–344). Hershey, PA: IGI Global. doi:10.4018/978-1-5225-3068-8.ch018

Brookfield, S. (2016). Using Narrative and Team-Teaching to Address Teaching About Racial Dynamics. In C. Scott & J. Sims (Eds.), *Developing Workforce Diversity Programs, Curriculum, and Degrees in Higher Education* (pp. 98–116). Hershey, PA: IGI Global. doi:10.4018/978-1-5225-0209-8.ch006

Related Readings

Byrd, M. Y., & Lloyd-Jones, B. (2016). Developing a Social Justice-Oriented Workforce Diversity Concentration in Human Relations Academic Programs. In C. Scott & J. Sims (Eds.), *Developing Workforce Diversity Programs, Curriculum, and Degrees in Higher Education* (pp. 179–196). Hershey, PA: IGI Global. doi:10.4018/978-1-5225-0209-8.ch010

Castillo-Page, L., Eliason, J., Conrad, S. S., & Nivet, M. A. (2016). Diversity in Undergraduate Medical Education: An Examination of Organizational Culture and Climate in Medical Schools. In C. Scott & J. Sims (Eds.), *Developing Workforce Diversity Programs, Curriculum, and Degrees in Higher Education* (pp. 304–326). Hershey, PA: IGI Global. doi:10.4018/978-1-5225-0209-8.ch016

Coffey, H., Harden, S. B., Byker, E. J., Good, A. J., & Fisher, L. B. (2018). Developing Self- and Cultural-Awareness Through Introductory Education Courses: The "Me" Semester. In D. Polly, M. Putman, T. Petty, & A. Good (Eds.), *Innovative Practices in Teacher Preparation and Graduate-Level Teacher Education Programs* (pp. 67–86). Hershey, PA: IGI Global. doi:10.4018/978-1-5225-3068-8.ch005

Dimitrov, N., & Haque, A. (2017). Intercultural Teaching Competence in the Disciplines: Teaching Strategies for Intercultural Learning. In G. García-Pérez & C. Rojas-Primus (Eds.), *Promoting Intercultural Communication Competencies in Higher Education* (pp. 89–118). Hershey, PA: IGI Global. doi:10.4018/978-1-5225-1732-0.ch004

Downton, M. P. (2018). Preparation for Future Teaching: Authentic Activities in a Teacher Education Classroom. In D. Polly, M. Putman, T. Petty, & A. Good (Eds.), *Innovative Practices in Teacher Preparation and Graduate-Level Teacher Education Programs* (pp. 293–305). Hershey, PA: IGI Global. doi:10.4018/978-1-5225-3068-8.ch016

Escobar, J. C. (2017). Target Language, Target Culture: Intercultural Competence in the SSL (Spanish as a Second Language) Classroom. In G. García-Pérez & C. Rojas-Primus (Eds.), *Promoting Intercultural Communication Competencies in Higher Education* (pp. 257–280). Hershey, PA: IGI Global. doi:10.4018/978-1-5225-1732-0.ch010

Evans, N. D. (2019). Connecting Higher Education Learning Spaces in a Blended Zululand Teaching and Learning Ecology. In J. Keengwe (Ed.), *Handbook of Research on Blended Learning Pedagogies and Professional Development in Higher Education* (pp. 177–195). Hershey, PA: IGI Global. doi:10.4018/978-1-5225-5557-5.ch010

Farmer, L. S. (2019). The Role of Librarians in Blended Courses. In J. Keengwe (Ed.), *Handbook of Research on Blended Learning Pedagogies and Professional Development in Higher Education* (pp. 122–138). Hershey, PA: IGI Global. doi:10.4018/978-1-5225-5557-5.ch007

Fedeli, L., & Pennazio, V. (2019). An Exploratory Study on Teacher Training: The Use and Impact of Technologies Within a Specialization Course for Special Needs. In B. Rice (Ed.), *Global Perspectives on Inclusive Teacher Education* (pp. 58–81). Hershey, PA: IGI Global. doi:10.4018/978-1-5225-7703-4.ch005

Ficarra, L. R., & Chapin, D. A. (2019). The Role of Course Management Systems (CMS) in Addressing Universal Design for Learning (UDL) in College Classrooms. In J. Keengwe (Ed.), *Handbook of Research on Blended Learning Pedagogies and Professional Development in Higher Education* (pp. 60–78). Hershey, PA: IGI Global. doi:10.4018/978-1-5225-5557-5.ch004

Fisher, M. H., Jong, C., Thomas, J., & Schack, E. O. (2018). Noticing Pre-Service Teachers' Attitudes Toward Mathematics in Traditional and Online Classrooms. In D. Polly, M. Putman, T. Petty, & A. Good (Eds.), *Innovative Practices in Teacher Preparation and Graduate-Level Teacher Education Programs* (pp. 123–133). Hershey, PA: IGI Global. doi:10.4018/978-1-5225-3068-8.ch008

Fraga, L. M., Foster, S. L., & Falcon, L. (2019). Model for My Students?: I'm Not Sure How to Integrate Technology Either! In J. Keengwe (Ed.), *Handbook of Research on Blended Learning Pedagogies and Professional Development in Higher Education* (pp. 274–289). Hershey, PA: IGI Global. doi:10.4018/978-1-5225-5557-5.ch015

Gaffney, M., & McAnelly, K. (2019). The Aotearoa New Zealand Curriculum Te Whāriki as a Basis for Developing Dispositions of Inclusion: Early Childhood Student Teachers Partnering With Families as Part of Their Pedagogical Practice. In B. Rice (Ed.), *Global Perspectives on Inclusive Teacher Education* (pp. 181–195). Hershey, PA: IGI Global. doi:10.4018/978-1-5225-7703-4.ch011

Garson, K. D. (2017). Internationalization and Intercultural Learning: A Mixed Methods Study. In G. García-Pérez & C. Rojas-Primus (Eds.), *Promoting Intercultural Communication Competencies in Higher Education* (pp. 54–88). Hershey, PA: IGI Global. doi:10.4018/978-1-5225-1732-0.ch003

Goodson-Espy, T. J., & Salinas, T. M. (2018). Synergistic Teacher Preparation: The Winding Road to Teaching Science and Mathematics in Rural Schools. In D. Polly, M. Putman, T. Petty, & A. Good (Eds.), *Innovative Practices in Teacher Preparation and Graduate-Level Teacher Education Programs* (pp. 345–367). Hershey, PA: IGI Global. doi:10.4018/978-1-5225-3068-8.ch019

Related Readings

Greer, B. M., Luethge, D. J., & Robinson, G. (2016). Utilizing Virtual Technology as a Tool to Enhance the Workforce Diversity Learning. In C. Scott & J. Sims (Eds.), *Developing Workforce Diversity Programs, Curriculum, and Degrees in Higher Education* (pp. 258–279). Hershey, PA: IGI Global. doi:10.4018/978-1-5225-0209-8.ch014

Gupta, T., Herrington, D., & Yezierski, E. J. (2018). Target Inquiry: A Case for Quality Professional Development. In D. Polly, M. Putman, T. Petty, & A. Good (Eds.), *Innovative Practices in Teacher Preparation and Graduate-Level Teacher Education Programs* (pp. 383–416). Hershey, PA: IGI Global. doi:10.4018/978-1-5225-3068-8.ch021

Hailu, M., Mackey, J., Pan, J., & Arend, B. D. (2017). Turning Good Intentions into Good Teaching: Five Common Principles for Culturally Responsive Pedagogy. In G. García-Pérez & C. Rojas-Primus (Eds.), *Promoting Intercultural Communication Competencies in Higher Education* (pp. 20–53). Hershey, PA: IGI Global. doi:10.4018/978-1-5225-1732-0.ch002

Han, S. J., Lim, D. H., & Jung, E. (2019). A Collaborative Active Learning Model as a Vehicle for Online Team Learning in Higher Education. In J. Keengwe (Ed.), *Handbook of Research on Blended Learning Pedagogies and Professional Development in Higher Education* (pp. 40–59). Hershey, PA: IGI Global. doi:10.4018/978-1-5225-5557-5.ch003

Hedegaard-Soerensen, L., & Hamre, B. F. (2019). Divergent Agendas Within the Danish School Policy and the Dilemmas This Creates for Teachers Working With Inclusive Education. In B. Rice (Ed.), *Global Perspectives on Inclusive Teacher Education* (pp. 246–259). Hershey, PA: IGI Global. doi:10.4018/978-1-5225-7703-4.ch015

Heineke, A. J., & Papola-Ellis, A. (2018). Field-Based Teacher Education to Promote All Students' Language and Literacy Development. In D. Polly, M. Putman, T. Petty, & A. Good (Eds.), *Innovative Practices in Teacher Preparation and Graduate-Level Teacher Education Programs* (pp. 238–261). Hershey, PA: IGI Global. doi:10.4018/978-1-5225-3068-8.ch014

Hendrix, T. J. (2019). Unconventional Delivery: Developing and Implementing Service-Learning in an Online Course. In J. Keengwe (Ed.), *Handbook of Research on Blended Learning Pedagogies and Professional Development in Higher Education* (pp. 259–273). Hershey, PA: IGI Global. doi:10.4018/978-1-5225-5557-5.ch014

Hickey, M. G. (2019). Burmese Refugee Students in U.S. Schools: What Educators Should Know. In B. Rice (Ed.), *Global Perspectives on Inclusive Teacher Education* (pp. 196–213). Hershey, PA: IGI Global. doi:10.4018/978-1-5225-7703-4.ch012

Hode, M. G., & Behm-Morawitz, E. (2016). Exploring the Impact of an Online Diversity Course for the Professional Development of Faculty and Staff. In C. Scott & J. Sims (Eds.), *Developing Workforce Diversity Programs, Curriculum, and Degrees in Higher Education* (pp. 1–27). Hershey, PA: IGI Global. doi:10.4018/978-1-5225-0209-8.ch001

Homp, M. (2019). Facilitating Active Learning and Collaboration in Online Mathematics Content Courses for Secondary Teachers. In J. Keengwe (Ed.), *Handbook of Research on Blended Learning Pedagogies and Professional Development in Higher Education* (pp. 139–155). Hershey, PA: IGI Global. doi:10.4018/978-1-5225-5557-5.ch008

Homsey, D. M. (2016). Organizational Socialization and Workplace Diversity: The Case for Experiential Learning. In C. Scott & J. Sims (Eds.), *Developing Workforce Diversity Programs, Curriculum, and Degrees in Higher Education* (pp. 197–209). Hershey, PA: IGI Global. doi:10.4018/978-1-5225-0209-8.ch011

Hundley, M., Palmeri, A., Hostetler, A., Johnson, H., Dunleavy, T. K., & Self, E. A. (2018). Developmental Trajectories, Disciplinary Practices, and Sites of Practice in Novice Teacher Learning: A Thing to Be Learned. In D. Polly, M. Putman, T. Petty, & A. Good (Eds.), *Innovative Practices in Teacher Preparation and Graduate-Level Teacher Education Programs* (pp. 153–180). Hershey, PA: IGI Global. doi:10.4018/978-1-5225-3068-8.ch010

Jacobsen, M., Friesen, S., & Brown, B. (2018). Teachers' Professional Learning Focused on Designs for Early Learners and Technology. In D. Polly, M. Putman, T. Petty, & A. Good (Eds.), *Innovative Practices in Teacher Preparation and Graduate-Level Teacher Education Programs* (pp. 417–438). Hershey, PA: IGI Global. doi:10.4018/978-1-5225-3068-8.ch022

Johnson, S., Conley, M., & Pope, M. L. (2016). Implementing Black Male Initiative Programs: A Model for Promoting African American Male Success at a Metropolitan University. In C. Scott & J. Sims (Eds.), *Developing Workforce Diversity Programs, Curriculum, and Degrees in Higher Education* (pp. 28–42). Hershey, PA: IGI Global. doi:10.4018/978-1-5225-0209-8.ch002

Related Readings

Jung, E. J. (2017). The Road to Intercultural Development and Internationalization. In G. García-Pérez & C. Rojas-Primus (Eds.), *Promoting Intercultural Communication Competencies in Higher Education* (pp. 1–19). Hershey, PA: IGI Global. doi:10.4018/978-1-5225-1732-0.ch001

Karataş, S., Kukul, V., & Özcan, S. (2018). How Powerful Is Digital Storytelling for Teaching?: Perspective of Pre-Service Teachers. In D. Polly, M. Putman, T. Petty, & A. Good (Eds.), *Innovative Practices in Teacher Preparation and Graduate-Level Teacher Education Programs* (pp. 511–529). Hershey, PA: IGI Global. doi:10.4018/978-1-5225-3068-8.ch027

Kurawa, G. (2019). Examining Teachers' Professional Development for Promoting Inclusive Education in Displacement. In B. Rice (Ed.), *Global Perspectives on Inclusive Teacher Education* (pp. 260–278). Hershey, PA: IGI Global. doi:10.4018/978-1-5225-7703-4.ch016

LaFever, M. (2017). Using the Medicine Wheel for Curriculum Design in Intercultural Communication: Rethinking Learning Outcomes. In G. García-Pérez & C. Rojas-Primus (Eds.), *Promoting Intercultural Communication Competencies in Higher Education* (pp. 168–199). Hershey, PA: IGI Global. doi:10.4018/978-1-5225-1732-0.ch007

Langford, C. L. (2016). Trans*Forming Higher Education to Advance Workforce Diversity. In C. Scott & J. Sims (Eds.), *Developing Workforce Diversity Programs, Curriculum, and Degrees in Higher Education* (pp. 211–234). Hershey, PA: IGI Global. doi:10.4018/978-1-5225-0209-8.ch012

Li, G. (2018). Moving Toward a Diversity Plus Teacher Education: Approaches, Challenges, and Possibilities in Preparing Teachers for English Language Learners. In D. Polly, M. Putman, T. Petty, & A. Good (Eds.), *Innovative Practices in Teacher Preparation and Graduate-Level Teacher Education Programs* (pp. 215–236). Hershey, PA: IGI Global. doi:10.4018/978-1-5225-3068-8.ch013

Lim, L., & Thaver, T. (2019). Disability Awareness in Teacher Education in Singapore. In B. Rice (Ed.), *Global Perspectives on Inclusive Teacher Education* (pp. 214–227). Hershey, PA: IGI Global. doi:10.4018/978-1-5225-7703-4.ch013

Lock, J. V., Johnson, C., Altowairiki, N., Burns, A., Hill, L., & Ostrowski, C. P. (2019). Enhancing Instructor Capacity Through the Redesign of Online Practicum Course Environments Using Universal Design for Learning. In J. Keengwe (Ed.), *Handbook of Research on Blended Learning Pedagogies and Professional Development in Higher Education* (pp. 1–20). Hershey, PA: IGI Global. doi:10.4018/978-1-5225-5557-5.ch001

López, J. S. (2017). Gender Divides in Higher Education: Awareness of Key Competencies in the Building Industry. In G. García-Pérez & C. Rojas-Primus (Eds.), *Promoting Intercultural Communication Competencies in Higher Education* (pp. 200–228). Hershey, PA: IGI Global. doi:10.4018/978-1-5225-1732-0.ch008

Machado, L., Klein, A. Z., Freitas, A., Schlemmer, E., & Pedron, C. D. (2016). The Use of Virtual Worlds for Developing Intercultural Competences. *International Journal of Information and Communication Technology Education, 12*(3), 51–64. doi:10.4018/IJICTE.2016070105

Magsamen-Conrad, K., Dillon, J. M., Hanasono, L. K., & Valdez, P. A. (2016). Developing an Intergroup Communication Intervention Curriculum: Enhancing Workforce Skills Across Generations. In C. Scott & J. Sims (Eds.), *Developing Workforce Diversity Programs, Curriculum, and Degrees in Higher Education* (pp. 140–161). Hershey, PA: IGI Global. doi:10.4018/978-1-5225-0209-8.ch008

Maher, D. (2019). The Use of Course Management Systems in Pre-Service Teacher Education. In J. Keengwe (Ed.), *Handbook of Research on Blended Learning Pedagogies and Professional Development in Higher Education* (pp. 196–213). Hershey, PA: IGI Global. doi:10.4018/978-1-5225-5557-5.ch011

Maiorescu, R. D., & Eberhardinger, M. J. (2016). A Future Direction for Integrating Workforce Diversity across the Curriculum: A Case Study of Strategic Planning, Interdisciplinary Research, and Co-Teaching. In C. Scott & J. Sims (Eds.), *Developing Workforce Diversity Programs, Curriculum, and Degrees in Higher Education* (pp. 327–343). Hershey, PA: IGI Global. doi:10.4018/978-1-5225-0209-8.ch017

Manzoor, A. (2018). Technology Tools for Building Diverse, Equitable, and Inclusive Classrooms. *International Journal of Technology and Educational Marketing, 8*(2), 75–94. doi:10.4018/IJTEM.2018070105

Matthews, J. J. (2016). A Perspective on How Counseling Curricula can Enhance Workforce Diversity Practices. In C. Scott & J. Sims (Eds.), *Developing Workforce Diversity Programs, Curriculum, and Degrees in Higher Education* (pp. 162–178). Hershey, PA: IGI Global. doi:10.4018/978-1-5225-0209-8.ch009

McCormack, V. F., Stauffer, M., Fishley, K., Hohenbrink, J., Mascazine, J. R., & Zigler, T. (2018). Designing a Dual Licensure Path for Middle Childhood and Special Education Teacher Candidates. In D. Polly, M. Putman, T. Petty, & A. Good (Eds.), *Innovative Practices in Teacher Preparation and Graduate-Level Teacher Education Programs* (pp. 21–36). Hershey, PA: IGI Global. doi:10.4018/978-1-5225-3068-8.ch002

Related Readings

Militello, M., Tredway, L., & Jones, K. D. (2019). A Reimagined EdD: Participatory, Progressive Online Pedagogy. In J. Keengwe (Ed.), *Handbook of Research on Blended Learning Pedagogies and Professional Development in Higher Education* (pp. 214–243). Hershey, PA: IGI Global. doi:10.4018/978-1-5225-5557-5.ch012

Mokher, C. G., Cavalluzzo, L., & Henderson, S. (2018). Examining Teachers' Instructional Practices as They Progress Through the National Board Certification Process. In D. Polly, M. Putman, T. Petty, & A. Good (Eds.), *Innovative Practices in Teacher Preparation and Graduate-Level Teacher Education Programs* (pp. 464–487). Hershey, PA: IGI Global. doi:10.4018/978-1-5225-3068-8.ch025

Moser, K., Zhu, D., Nguyen, H., & Williams, E. (2018). Teaching English Language Learners: A Mainstream Response to Rural Teacher Preparation. *International Journal of Teacher Education and Professional Development*, *1*(1), 58–75. doi:10.4018/IJTEPD.2018010105

Munger, M. H., Murray, M., Richardson, M., & Claussen, A. (2018). Transformative Learning in Teacher Education: Literature as a Bridge for Increasing Cultural Competence. *International Journal of Adult Vocational Education and Technology*, *9*(4), 54–64. doi:10.4018/IJAVET.2018100105

Naranjo, J. (2018). Meeting the Need for Inclusive Educators Online: Teacher Education in Inclusive Special Education and Dual-Certification. In D. Polly, M. Putman, T. Petty, & A. Good (Eds.), *Innovative Practices in Teacher Preparation and Graduate-Level Teacher Education Programs* (pp. 106–122). Hershey, PA: IGI Global. doi:10.4018/978-1-5225-3068-8.ch007

Ngigi, S. K., & Obura, E. A. (2019). Blended Learning in Higher Education: Challenges and Opportunities. In J. Keengwe (Ed.), *Handbook of Research on Blended Learning Pedagogies and Professional Development in Higher Education* (pp. 290–306). Hershey, PA: IGI Global. doi:10.4018/978-1-5225-5557-5.ch016

Ntuli, E. (2018). Instructional Technology Courses in Teacher Education: A Study of Inservice Teachers' Perceptions and Recommendations. *International Journal of Information and Communication Technology Education*, *14*(3), 41–54. doi:10.4018/IJICTE.2018070104

Palahicky, S., DesBiens, D., Jeffery, K., & Webster, K. S. (2019). Pedagogical Values in Online and Blended Learning Environments in Higher Education. In J. Keengwe (Ed.), *Handbook of Research on Blended Learning Pedagogies and Professional Development in Higher Education* (pp. 79–101). Hershey, PA: IGI Global. doi:10.4018/978-1-5225-5557-5.ch005

Penland, J. L., Laviers, K., Bassham, E., & Nnochiri, V. (2019). Virtual Learning: A Study of Virtual Reality for Distance Education. In J. Keengwe (Ed.), *Handbook of Research on Blended Learning Pedagogies and Professional Development in Higher Education* (pp. 156–176). Hershey, PA: IGI Global. doi:10.4018/978-1-5225-5557-5.ch009

Plakhotnik, M. S. (2017). Understanding Social Identity through Autoethography: Building Intercultural Communication Competencies in Higher Education Classroom. In G. García-Pérez & C. Rojas-Primus (Eds.), *Promoting Intercultural Communication Competencies in Higher Education* (pp. 140–167). Hershey, PA: IGI Global. doi:10.4018/978-1-5225-1732-0.ch006

Pourreau, L., & Lokey-Vega, A. (2018). K-12 Virtual Educator Preparation: Insights and Inquiry. In D. Polly, M. Putman, T. Petty, & A. Good (Eds.), *Innovative Practices in Teacher Preparation and Graduate-Level Teacher Education Programs* (pp. 557–578). Hershey, PA: IGI Global. doi:10.4018/978-1-5225-3068-8.ch029

Prion, S., & Mitchell, M. (2019). Content Considerations for Blended Learning Experiences. In J. Keengwe (Ed.), *Handbook of Research on Blended Learning Pedagogies and Professional Development in Higher Education* (pp. 102–121). Hershey, PA: IGI Global. doi:10.4018/978-1-5225-5557-5.ch006

Pucella, T. J. (2018). Using the edTPA as a Formative and Summative Assessment Tool. In D. Polly, M. Putman, T. Petty, & A. Good (Eds.), *Innovative Practices in Teacher Preparation and Graduate-Level Teacher Education Programs* (pp. 181–199). Hershey, PA: IGI Global. doi:10.4018/978-1-5225-3068-8.ch011

Ragnarsdóttir, H. (2018). Perspectives on Equity, Inclusion, and Social Justice in Education in Four Nordic Countries. *International Journal of Bias, Identity and Diversities in Education*, *3*(2), 1–14. doi:10.4018/IJBIDE.2018070101

Ragoonaden, K. (2017). The Common European Framework of Reference for Languages, the Intercultural Development Index, and Intercultural Communication Competence. In G. García-Pérez & C. Rojas-Primus (Eds.), *Promoting Intercultural Communication Competencies in Higher Education* (pp. 281–306). Hershey, PA: IGI Global. doi:10.4018/978-1-5225-1732-0.ch011

Rangara-Omol, T. (2019). Understanding Student Support: The Link Between Faculty, Student, and Online Learning. In J. Keengwe (Ed.), *Handbook of Research on Blended Learning Pedagogies and Professional Development in Higher Education* (pp. 307–324). Hershey, PA: IGI Global. doi:10.4018/978-1-5225-5557-5.ch017

Related Readings

Re'vell, M. D. (2019). Moving Toward Culturally Restorative Teaching Exchanges: Using Restorative Practices to Develop Literacy Across Subject Area-Content. *International Journal of Smart Education and Urban Society, 10*(2), 53–69. doi:10.4018/IJSEUS.2019040104

Reynolds, H. M., & Wagle, A. T. (2018). Utilizing Program Specific Data to Develop Case Studies for Use With Preservice Teachers. In D. Polly, M. Putman, T. Petty, & A. Good (Eds.), *Innovative Practices in Teacher Preparation and Graduate-Level Teacher Education Programs* (pp. 1–20). Hershey, PA: IGI Global. doi:10.4018/978-1-5225-3068-8.ch001

Rhodes, C. M. (2018). Culturally Responsive Teaching with Adult Learners: A Review of the Literature. *International Journal of Adult Vocational Education and Technology, 9*(4), 33–41. doi:10.4018/IJAVET.2018100103

Rice, B. M. (2019). Finding Their Voice: Action Research and Autoethnography in Inclusive Teacher Preparation. In B. Rice (Ed.), *Global Perspectives on Inclusive Teacher Education* (pp. 16–29). Hershey, PA: IGI Global. doi:10.4018/978-1-5225-7703-4.ch002

Rotich, J. P., & Elliott, G. (2019). Teaching First Aid, CPR, and AED Using Blended Learning in Academic Settings. In J. Keengwe (Ed.), *Handbook of Research on Blended Learning Pedagogies and Professional Development in Higher Education* (pp. 325–339). Hershey, PA: IGI Global. doi:10.4018/978-1-5225-5557-5.ch018

Royal, W. A. (2017). The Philosopher's Teahouse: Building Intercultural Competency among Students. In G. García-Pérez & C. Rojas-Primus (Eds.), *Promoting Intercultural Communication Competencies in Higher Education* (pp. 229–256). Hershey, PA: IGI Global. doi:10.4018/978-1-5225-1732-0.ch009

Rudstam, H., Golden, T., Bruyere, S., Van Looy, S., & Gower, W. S. (2016). Beyond Handicap, Pity, and Inspiration: Disability and Diversity in Workforce Development Education and Practice. In C. Scott & J. Sims (Eds.), *Developing Workforce Diversity Programs, Curriculum, and Degrees in Higher Education* (pp. 280–303). Hershey, PA: IGI Global. doi:10.4018/978-1-5225-0209-8.ch015

Salinas, T. M., & Lynch-Davis, K. (2018). Using the PRIME Leadership Framework to Support Emerging Leaders in a Professional Development Project. In D. Polly, M. Putman, T. Petty, & A. Good (Eds.), *Innovative Practices in Teacher Preparation and Graduate-Level Teacher Education Programs* (pp. 439–449). Hershey, PA: IGI Global. doi:10.4018/978-1-5225-3068-8.ch023

Sanders, S. L., & Orbe, M. P. (2016). TIPs to Maximize Meaningful Professional Development Programs and Initiatives: A Case Study in Theoretically-Grounded Diversity Education. In C. Scott & J. Sims (Eds.), *Developing Workforce Diversity Programs, Curriculum, and Degrees in Higher Education* (pp. 235–257). Hershey, PA: IGI Global. doi:10.4018/978-1-5225-0209-8.ch013

Savva, S. (2019). Multiliteracies Professional Development Practice: Design and Evaluation of an Online Professional Development Program to Support Inclusive Teaching. In B. Rice (Ed.), *Global Perspectives on Inclusive Teacher Education* (pp. 156–179). Hershey, PA: IGI Global. doi:10.4018/978-1-5225-7703-4.ch010

Schroth, S. T., & Helfer, J. A. (2018). Differentiated Fieldwork and Practicum Experiences: Matching Teacher Candidate Assignments to Their Skills and Needs. In D. Polly, M. Putman, T. Petty, & A. Good (Eds.), *Innovative Practices in Teacher Preparation and Graduate-Level Teacher Education Programs* (pp. 306–326). Hershey, PA: IGI Global. doi:10.4018/978-1-5225-3068-8.ch017

Scott, C. L. (2016). The Diverse Voices Conference: Expanding Diversity Education Beyond the Classroom. In C. Scott, & J. Sims (Eds.), *Developing Workforce Diversity Programs, Curriculum, and Degrees in Higher Education* (pp. 62-73). Hershey, PA: IGI Global. doi:10.4018/978-1-5225-0209-8.ch004

Scott, J. A., Dostal, H. M., & Ewen-Smith, T. N. (2019). Inclusion and Exclusion: Global Challenges Within Deaf Education. In B. Rice (Ed.), *Global Perspectives on Inclusive Teacher Education* (pp. 120–136). Hershey, PA: IGI Global. doi:10.4018/978-1-5225-7703-4.ch008

Scribner, S., & Cartier, M. E. (2019). Thinking Outside the Box: Using Virtual Platforms to Collaboratively Co-Plan Effective and Engaging Instruction. In B. Rice (Ed.), *Global Perspectives on Inclusive Teacher Education* (pp. 43–57). Hershey, PA: IGI Global. doi:10.4018/978-1-5225-7703-4.ch004

Shambaugh, N. (2019). Applying a Teaching Decision Cycle to the Design of Online Learning Within Faculty Professional Development. In J. Keengwe (Ed.), *Handbook of Research on Blended Learning Pedagogies and Professional Development in Higher Education* (pp. 21–39). Hershey, PA: IGI Global. doi:10.4018/978-1-5225-5557-5.ch002

Shorter, S. (2016). Black Student-Faculty Mentorship Programs: A Means to Increase Workforce Diversity in the Professoriate. In C. Scott & J. Sims (Eds.), *Developing Workforce Diversity Programs, Curriculum, and Degrees in Higher Education* (pp. 43–61). Hershey, PA: IGI Global. doi:10.4018/978-1-5225-0209-8.ch003

Related Readings

Sims, A. (2016). Workforce Diversity Curriculum Design Considerations for Diversity Certificates and Study Abroad Experiences. In C. Scott & J. Sims (Eds.), *Developing Workforce Diversity Programs, Curriculum, and Degrees in Higher Education* (pp. 117–139). Hershey, PA: IGI Global. doi:10.4018/978-1-5225-0209-8.ch007

Sims, J. D., Shuff, J., Lai, H., Lim, O. F., Neese, A., Neese, S., & Sims, A. (2016). Diverse Student Scholars: How a Faculty Member's Undergraduate Research Program Can Advance Workforce Diversity Learning. In C. Scott & J. Sims (Eds.), *Developing Workforce Diversity Programs, Curriculum, and Degrees in Higher Education* (pp. 74–96). Hershey, PA: IGI Global. doi:10.4018/978-1-5225-0209-8.ch005

Skelcher, S. (2017). Cultural Conceptions of Flipped Learning: Examining Asian Perspectives in the 21st Century. *International Journal of Information and Communication Technology Education*, *13*(4), 17–27. doi:10.4018/IJICTE.2017100102

Soldner, J. L., Peter, D., Sajadi, S., & Paiewonsky, M. (2019). Evidence-Based Transition Practices: Implications for Local and Global Curriculum. In B. Rice (Ed.), *Global Perspectives on Inclusive Teacher Education* (pp. 98–119). Hershey, PA: IGI Global. doi:10.4018/978-1-5225-7703-4.ch007

Staley, C., Kenyon, R. S., & Marcovitz, D. M. (2018). Embedded Services: Going Beyond the Field of Dreams Model for Online Programs. In D. Polly, M. Putman, T. Petty, & A. Good (Eds.), *Innovative Practices in Teacher Preparation and Graduate-Level Teacher Education Programs* (pp. 368–381). Hershey, PA: IGI Global. doi:10.4018/978-1-5225-3068-8.ch020

Stapleton, J. N., Cuthrell, K. C., Tschida, C. M., & Fogarty, E. A. (2018). The PDSA Overhaul: Approaching Reform in Teacher Candidate Support. In D. Polly, M. Putman, T. Petty, & A. Good (Eds.), *Innovative Practices in Teacher Preparation and Graduate-Level Teacher Education Programs* (pp. 87–105). Hershey, PA: IGI Global. doi:10.4018/978-1-5225-3068-8.ch006

Stoicovy, C. E., & Rivera, M. N. (2019). Digital Storytelling as a Culturally Responsive Instructional Strategy for Pacific Islanders in Guam and Micronesia. *International Journal of Online Pedagogy and Course Design*, *9*(2), 33–43. doi:10.4018/IJOPCD.2019040103

Stone-MacDonald, A., & Shehaghilo, J. R. (2019). Assessment and Culturally Relevant Inclusive Education: The Case of Tanzania. In B. Rice (Ed.), *Global Perspectives on Inclusive Teacher Education* (pp. 228–245). Hershey, PA: IGI Global. doi:10.4018/978-1-5225-7703-4.ch014

Suh, J. M., & Gallagher, M. A. (2018). Preservice Teachers Decomposing Ambitious Mathematics Teaching: Video Analysis and Professional Learning Communities. In D. Polly, M. Putman, T. Petty, & A. Good (Eds.), *Innovative Practices in Teacher Preparation and Graduate-Level Teacher Education Programs* (pp. 37–47). Hershey, PA: IGI Global. doi:10.4018/978-1-5225-3068-8.ch003

Swartz, B. A., Lynch, J. M., & Lynch, S. D. (2018). Embedding Elementary Teacher Education Coursework in Local Classrooms: Examples in Mathematics and Special Education. In D. Polly, M. Putman, T. Petty, & A. Good (Eds.), *Innovative Practices in Teacher Preparation and Graduate-Level Teacher Education Programs* (pp. 262–292). Hershey, PA: IGI Global. doi:10.4018/978-1-5225-3068-8.ch015

Taraban-Gordon, S., & Page, E. (2017). Integrating Intercultural Competencies into the Professional Skills Curriculum. In G. García-Pérez & C. Rojas-Primus (Eds.), *Promoting Intercultural Communication Competencies in Higher Education* (pp. 119–139). Hershey, PA: IGI Global. doi:10.4018/978-1-5225-1732-0.ch005

Torff, B. (2018). Developmental Changes in Teachers' Attitudes About Professional Development. In D. Polly, M. Putman, T. Petty, & A. Good (Eds.), *Innovative Practices in Teacher Preparation and Graduate-Level Teacher Education Programs* (pp. 450–463). Hershey, PA: IGI Global. doi:10.4018/978-1-5225-3068-8.ch024

Vega, J. A., Arquette, C. M., Lee, H., Crowe, H. A., Hunzicker, J. L., & Cushing, J. (2018). Ensuring Social Justice for English Language Learners: An Innovative English as a Second Language (ESL) Endorsement Program. In D. Polly, M. Putman, T. Petty, & A. Good (Eds.), *Innovative Practices in Teacher Preparation and Graduate-Level Teacher Education Programs* (pp. 48–66). Hershey, PA: IGI Global. doi:10.4018/978-1-5225-3068-8.ch004

Viglietti, J. M., & Moore-Russo, D. (2018). Digital Resources for Mathematics Teachers: A Brave New World. In D. Polly, M. Putman, T. Petty, & A. Good (Eds.), *Innovative Practices in Teacher Preparation and Graduate-Level Teacher Education Programs* (pp. 489–510). Hershey, PA: IGI Global. doi:10.4018/978-1-5225-3068-8.ch026

Vorkapić, S. T., & Prović, P. (2018). Positive Psychology Competences of Pre-School Teachers as a Tool for Understanding and Nurturing Children's Play. In D. Polly, M. Putman, T. Petty, & A. Good (Eds.), *Innovative Practices in Teacher Preparation and Graduate-Level Teacher Education Programs* (pp. 134–152). Hershey, PA: IGI Global. doi:10.4018/978-1-5225-3068-8.ch009

Related Readings

Ward-Jackson, J., & Yu, C. (2019). Impact of Online Learning in K-12: Effectiveness, Challenges, and Limitations for Online Instruction. In J. Keengwe (Ed.), *Handbook of Research on Blended Learning Pedagogies and Professional Development in Higher Education* (pp. 357–375). Hershey, PA: IGI Global. doi:10.4018/978-1-5225-5557-5.ch020

Whitburn, B., & Corcoran, T. (2019). Ontologies of Inclusion and Teacher Education. In B. Rice (Ed.), *Global Perspectives on Inclusive Teacher Education* (pp. 1–15). Hershey, PA: IGI Global. doi:10.4018/978-1-5225-7703-4.ch001

Williams, Y. (2019). Building a Conceptual Framework for Culturally Inclusive Collaboration for Urban Practitioners. In B. Rice (Ed.), *Global Perspectives on Inclusive Teacher Education* (pp. 83–97). Hershey, PA: IGI Global. doi:10.4018/978-1-5225-7703-4.ch006

Woodley, X. M., Mucundanyi, G., & Lockard, M. (2017). Designing Counter-Narratives: Constructing Culturally Responsive Curriculum Online. *International Journal of Online Pedagogy and Course Design*, 7(1), 43–56. doi:10.4018/IJOPCD.2017010104

Yildiz, M. N., & Palak, D. (2016). Cultivating Global Competencies for the 21st Century Classroom: A Transformative Teaching Model. *International Journal of Information Communication Technologies and Human Development*, 8(1), 69–77. doi:10.4018/IJICTHD.2016010104

Ziliak, E. M. (2019). Calculus 1 Course Comparison: Online/Blended or Flipped? In J. Keengwe (Ed.), *Handbook of Research on Blended Learning Pedagogies and Professional Development in Higher Education* (pp. 244–258). Hershey, PA: IGI Global. doi:10.4018/978-1-5225-5557-5.ch013

About the Contributors

Uri Shafrir is associate professor in the Department of Human Development and Applied Psychology, and Director of Adult Study Skills Clinic at Ontario Institute for Studies in Education at the University of Toronto. His recent research focuses on enhancing learning outcomes with pedagogy for conceptual thinking with Meaning Equivalence Reusable Learning Objects (MERLO) and Post-Failure Reflectivity (PFR) for deep comprehension of conceptual content. Shafrir received a doctorate in mathematical sciences from the University of California at Los Angeles in 1962 and a doctorate in developmental psychology from York University, Toronto, in 1987. Before moving to the University of Toronto, he was founder and director of the Institute of Planetary and Space Science at Tel-Aviv University, and Adjunct Professor at the University of Wisconsin and Columbia University.

* * *

Joana Aguiar has been part of the concept mapping research group at University of São Paulo (Brazil) since 2010. She gained her PhD in Science Education (2018) working on 'map shock' - excessive cognitive load due to format and/or content caused by concept maps prepared by Chemistry teachers. Joana was part of the organizing committee of the Sixth and Eight International Conferences on Concept Mapping.

Paola Carante has a PhD in mathematics education, held at the University of Torino, in Italy. She worked with professors O. Robutti and F. Arzarello as supervisors. Her research interests focus on mathematics teachers' professional development, working in communities and collaborating with researchers to design new instructional resources for the mathematics teaching, learning and assessing. Paola has experience in teaching at secondary schools and at the beginning of University. She is involved in national and international research projects (MERLO project and PLS), aimed at improving and promoting the study of scientific disciplines. During the last years, she participated in national and international conferences (e.g. PME, ICME, CIEAEM), presenting papers.

About the Contributors

Paulo Rogério Miranda Correia is Professor within the School of Arts, Sciences and Humanities at the University of São Paulo (USP). He has been involved in research on concept mapping applied to teaching and learning since 2006. His current research aims to understand how to optimize the use of concept mapping in considering human cognitive architecture. Paulo was the chairman of the Sixth International Conference on Concept Mapping (CMC2014) organized by USP and the Institute for Human and Machine Cognition (IHMC).

Ron Kenett is Chairman of the KPA Group, Israel, Senior Research Fellow at the Neaman Institute, Technion, Haifa and Visiting Professor at the Institute for Drug Research at the School of Medicine of the Hebrew University of Jerusalem, Israel. He is an applied statistician combining expertise in academic, consulting and business domains. Ron is Past President of the Israel Statistical Association (ISA) and of the European Network for Business and Industrial Statistics (ENBIS). He authored and co-authored over 250 papers and 14 books on topics such as biostatistics, healthcare, industrial statistics, customer surveys, multivariate quality control, risk management and information quality. The KPA Group he founded in 1994, is a leading Israeli firm focused on generating insights through analytics. He is editor in chief of Wiley's StatsRef, serves on the editorial board of several international journals and was awarded the 2013 Greenfield Medal by the Royal Statistical Society and, in 2018, The Box Medal from the European Network for Business and Industrial Statistics. He is member of the National Public Advisory Council for Statistics Israel and member of the Executive Academic Council, Wingate Academic College. He founded the point and click translator company, Babylon.com and is member of the board of several startup companies. His book, titled Information Quality (InfoQ): The Potential of Data and Analytics to Generate Knowledge, is dealing with the design of data science programs and is addressing the issue of reproducibility in scientific research. Ron holds a BSc in Mathematics (with first class honors) from Imperial College, London University and a PhD in Mathematics from the Weizmann Institute of Science, Rehovot, Israel.

Brian Moon is the founder of Chief Technology Officer for Perigean Technologies and founder and President of Sero! Learning Assessments, Inc. As the inventor of Sero!, Mr. Moon is working to enable the assessment of learning using concept maps, for efficient classroom and large-scale use. A leading practitioner and researcher in the fields of expertise management and cognitive systems engineering, Mr. Moon applies diagrammatic and naturalistic interviewing techniques to elicit, protect, enable and assess expert knowledge. His practice enables expertise management, design and evaluation of cognitive systems, and the assessment of knowledge. He is widely recognized for his innovative applications of concept mapping, which are highlighted in the edited volume, Applied Concept Mapping: Capturing, Analyzing, and Organizing Knowledge. His clients have included numerous Fortune 500 companies, the Advanced Distributed Learning Initiative, Veterans Administration, the US Department of Defense.

Theodosia Prodromou (PhD, MSc, MA, BSc (Hons), DipTeach, DipArt, GCTE) is a Cypriot-Australian mathematician, statistician and mathematics educator, who joined the University of New England in Australia in July 2009 after completing her PhD studies at Warwick university in United kingdom. She taught primary and secondary Mathematics in different countries of Europe, and Australia. She has experience of teaching mathematics education to pre-service teachers and in-service teachers within primary, secondary and post-graduate programs. She is involved in European and International research projects. She is the chair of the GeoGebra institute in Australia. Her interests mostly focus on: the relationship between technology and mathematical thinking; integration of digital technologies in the teaching of mathematics; STEM education; Secondary teachers' professional development; statistics education, statistical literacy, use of Big Data in Educational settings. She is working on numerous research projects worldwide related to technology integration into schools; Big Data and Augmented Reality.

Ornella Robutti is Associate Professor in Mathematics Education at the Department of Mathematics of the University of Torino. Her fields of research are: the teaching and learning cognitive processes in Mathematics with the support of technologies; the professional role of mathematics teachers as individuals and in communities; meanings of mathematical objects and their construction. She is author of articles and book chapters in her research fields and present as team leader/lecturer/participant in many international congresses (PME, CERME, CIEAEM, CADGME, ICME). In Italy she is member of CIIM Commission (http://www.umi-ciim.it/) in UMI (Italian Mathematical Union), the person in charge of: the GeoGebra Institute of Turin, the project of teachers' professional development Piano Lauree Scientifiche in Piedmont; the project Liceo Matematico; the national congress DIFIMA; and she has been member of Scientific committees of national programmes with technologies: m@t.abel, PON-m@t.abel.

Index

A

assessment 4-5, 7-8, 10, 18, 22, 25-27, 30, 38-39, 42-44, 47-48, 59, 62-63, 67-68, 78-80, 82, 87, 92, 94-95, 100, 117, 119-122, 126-129

C

caesarean surgery 87, 93, 95, 112
concept mapping 11, 26-27, 94, 117, 119, 121, 131
Conceptual curation 23-24, 56
conceptual thinking 1-2, 6, 8, 11, 17-19, 22, 38-39, 48, 54, 56, 62, 92
concordance 54, 56, 87, 100, 103, 108, 112, 115
concordance analysis 87, 100, 112
correlation 99, 103, 115
creative design process 1

D

deep learning 119

E

enhance comprehension 87, 91, 112
Enhanced Learning Outcomes 19, 26, 38
Evidence-Based Informed Consent (EBIC) 86, 115

F

feedback 29-30, 33, 35, 39, 48, 52, 117, 119, 127-129

G

gynecology 88, 91, 93

H

hierarchical clustering 86, 97-99, 105-106, 116
higher education 19
higher order thinking 19

J

joint probability 87, 100-101, 107-108

K

Kappa agreement 86, 97, 102-103
Kappa Statistic 116

L

Learning From Precedent 6

M

mathematics education 61-62, 64, 66, 68, 70-71, 75-76, 81

Meaning Equivalence 1-3, 5-9, 11-13, 15, 18-19, 22, 24-26, 30-31, 35, 38-42, 45, 47-48, 61-62, 64-65, 78, 82, 86-87, 91-92, 95, 116
Meaning Equivalence Reusable Learning Object (MERLO) 38

O

Ordinal Data 99, 116

P

pedagogic resonance 129
pedagogy for conceptual thinking 1-2, 6, 11, 19, 22, 38-39, 48, 54, 56
praxeologies 61-64, 66, 68, 73, 75-82
problematic knowledge 119, 130

production scores 16, 18, 86, 98, 100, 103-109, 111

R

recognition scores 100, 103-105, 107-109, 111-112

S

Sero! 117, 119, 121, 123
statistics 7, 25, 30, 33, 37, 57, 59, 97, 103, 122

T

teachers' professional development 62
threshold concepts 119, 130

Purchase Print, E-Book, or Print + E-Book

IGI Global's reference books can now be purchased from three unique pricing formats:
Print Only, E-Book Only, or Print + E-Book.
Shipping fees may apply.

www.igi-global.com

Recommended Reference Books

ISBN: 978-1-5225-9348-5
© 2019; 454 pp.
List Price: $255

ISBN: 978-1-5225-7763-8
© 2019; 253 pp.
List Price: $175

ISBN: 978-1-5225-7531-3
© 2019; 324 pp.
List Price: $185

ISBN: 978-1-5225-7802-4
© 2019; 423 pp.
List Price: $195

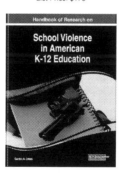

ISBN: 978-1-5225-6246-7
© 2019; 610 pp.
List Price: $275

ISBN: 978-1-5225-2998-9
© 2018; 352 pp.
List Price: $195

Looking for free content, product updates, news, and special offers?
Join IGI Global's mailing list today and start enjoying exclusive perks sent only to IGI Global members.
Add your name to the list at **www.igi-global.com/newsletters**.

Publisher of Peer-Reviewed, Timely, and Innovative Academic Research

IGI Global
DISSEMINATOR of KNOWLEDGE

www.igi-global.com ✉ Sign up at www.igi-global.com/newsletters f facebook.com/igiglobal t twitter.com/igiglobal

Ensure Quality Research is Introduced to the Academic Community

Become an IGI Global Reviewer for Authored Book Projects

 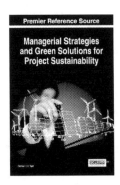  

The overall success of an authored book project is dependent on quality and timely reviews.

In this competitive age of scholarly publishing, constructive and timely feedback significantly expedites the turnaround time of manuscripts from submission to acceptance, allowing the publication and discovery of forward-thinking research at a much more expeditious rate. Several IGI Global authored book projects are currently seeking highly-qualified experts in the field to fill vacancies on their respective editorial review boards:

Applications and Inquiries may be sent to:
development@igi-global.com

Applicants must have a doctorate (or an equivalent degree) as well as publishing and reviewing experience. Reviewers are asked to complete the open-ended evaluation questions with as much detail as possible in a timely, collegial, and constructive manner. All reviewers' tenures run for one-year terms on the editorial review boards and are expected to complete at least three reviews per term. Upon successful completion of this term, reviewers can be considered for an additional term.

If you have a colleague that may be interested in this opportunity, we encourage you to share this information with them.

IGI Global Proudly Partners With eContent Pro International

Receive a 25% Discount on all Editorial Services

Editorial Services

IGI Global expects all final manuscripts submitted for publication to be in their final form. This means they must be reviewed, revised, and professionally copy edited prior to their final submission. Not only does this support with accelerating the publication process, but it also ensures that the highest quality scholarly work can be disseminated.

English Language Copy Editing

Let eContent Pro International's expert copy editors perform edits on your manuscript to resolve spelling, punctuaion, grammar, syntax, flow, formatting issues and more.

Scientific and Scholarly Editing

Allow colleagues in your research area to examine the content of your manuscript and provide you with valuable feedback and suggestions before submission.

Figure, Table, Chart & Equation Conversions

Do you have poor quality figures? Do you need visual elements in your manuscript created or converted? A design expert can help!

Translation

Need your documjent translated into English? eContent Pro International's expert translators are fluent in English and more than 40 different languages.

Hear What Your Colleagues are Saying About Editorial Services Supported by IGI Global

"The service was very fast, very thorough, and very helpful in ensuring our chapter meets the criteria and requirements of the book's editors. I was quite impressed and happy with your service."

– Prof. Tom Brinthaupt,
Middle Tennessee State University, USA

"I found the work actually spectacular. The editing, formatting, and other checks were very thorough. The turnaround time was great as well. I will definitely use eContent Pro in the future."

– Nickanor Amwata, Lecturer,
University of Kurdistan Hawler, Iraq

"I was impressed that it was done timely, and wherever the content was not clear for the reader, the paper was improved with better readability for the audience."

– Prof. James Chilembwe,
Mzuzu University, Malawi

Email: customerservice@econtentpro.com   www.igi-global.com/editorial-service-partners

Celebrating Over 30 Years of Scholarly Knowledge Creation & Dissemination

www.igi-global.com

InfoSci®-Books

A Database of Over 5,300+ Reference Books Containing Over 100,000+ Chapters Focusing on Emerging Research

GAIN ACCESS TO **THOUSANDS** OF REFERENCE BOOKS AT **A FRACTION** OF THEIR INDIVIDUAL LIST **PRICE**.

InfoSci®-Books Database

The **InfoSci®-Books** database is a collection of over 5,300+ IGI Global single and multi-volume reference books, handbooks of research, and encyclopedias, encompassing groundbreaking research from prominent experts worldwide that span over 350+ topics in 11 core subject areas including business, computer science, education, science and engineering, social sciences and more.

Open Access Fee Waiver (Offset Model) Initiative

For any library that invests in IGI Global's InfoSci-Journals and/or InfoSci-Books databases, IGI Global will match the library's investment with a fund of equal value to go toward **subsidizing the OA article processing charges (APCs) for their students, faculty, and staff** at that institution when their work is submitted and accepted under OA into an IGI Global journal.*

INFOSCI® PLATFORM FEATURES

- No DRM
- No Set-Up or Maintenance Fees
- A Guarantee of No More Than a 5% Annual Increase
- Full-Text HTML and PDF Viewing Options
- Downloadable MARC Records
- Unlimited Simultaneous Access
- COUNTER 5 Compliant Reports
- Formatted Citations With Ability to Export to RefWorks and EasyBib
- No Embargo of Content (Research is Available Months in Advance of the Print Release)

*The fund will be offered on an annual basis and expire at the end of the subscription period. The fund would renew as the subscription is renewed for each year thereafter. The open access fees will be waived after the student, faculty, or staff's paper has been vetted and accepted into an IGI Global journal and the fund can only be used toward publishing OA in an IGI Global journal. Libraries in developing countries will have the match on their investment doubled.

To Learn More or To Purchase This Database:
www.igi-global.com/infosci-books

eresources@igi-global.com • Toll Free: 1-866-342-6657 ext. 100 • Phone: 717-533-8845 x100

www.igi-global.com

Publisher of Peer-Reviewed, Timely, and
Innovative Academic Research Since 1988

IGI Global's Transformative Open Access (OA) Model:
How to Turn Your University Library's Database Acquisitions Into a Source of OA Funding

In response to the OA movement and well in advance of Plan S, IGI Global, early last year, unveiled their OA Fee Waiver (Offset Model) Initiative.

Under this initiative, librarians who invest in IGI Global's InfoSci-Books (5,300+ reference books) and/or InfoSci-Journals (185+ scholarly journals) databases will be able to subsidize their patron's OA article processing charges (APC) when their work is submitted and accepted (after the peer review process) into an IGI Global journal.*

How Does it Work?

1. When a library subscribes or perpetually purchases IGI Global's InfoSci-Databases including InfoSci-Books (5,300+ e-books), InfoSci-Journals (185+ e-journals), and/or their discipline/subject-focused subsets, IGI Global will match the library's investment with a fund of equal value to go toward subsidizing the OA article processing charges (APCs) for their patrons.

    Researchers: Be sure to recommend the InfoSci-Books and InfoSci-Journals to take advantage of this initiative.

2. When a student, faculty, or staff member submits a paper and it is accepted (following the peer review) into one of IGI Global's 185+ scholarly journals, the author will have the option to have their paper published under a traditional publishing model or as OA.

3. When the author chooses to have their paper published under OA, IGI Global will notify them of the OA Fee Waiver (Offset Model) Initiative. If the author decides they would like to take advantage of this initiative, IGI Global will deduct the US$ 1,500 APC from the created fund.

4. This fund will be offered on an annual basis and will renew as the subscription is renewed for each year thereafter. IGI Global will manage the fund and award the APC waivers unless the librarian has a preference as to how the funds should be managed.

Hear From the Experts on This Initiative:

"I'm very happy to have been able to make one of my recent research contributions, 'Visualizing the Social Media Conversations of a National Information Technology Professional Association' featured in the *International Journal of Human Capital and Information Technology Professionals*, freely available along with having access to the valuable resources found within IGI Global's InfoSci-Journals database."

– **Prof. Stuart Palmer**,
Deakin University, Australia

For More Information, Visit: www.igi-global.com/publish/contributor-resources/open-access or contact IGI Global's Database Team at eresources@igi-global.com

www.igi-global.com/infosci-ondemand

InfoSci®-OnDemand

Continuously updated with new material on a weekly basis, InfoSci®-OnDemand offers the ability to search through thousands of quality full-text research papers. Users can narrow each search by identifying key topic areas of interest, then display a complete listing of relevant papers, and purchase materials specific to their research needs.

Comprehensive Service
- Over 125,000+ journal articles, book chapters, and case studies.
- All content is downloadable in PDF and HTML format and can be stored locally for future use.

No Subscription Fees
- One time fee of $37.50 per PDF download.

Instant Access
- Receive a download link immediately after order completion!

"It really provides an excellent entry into the research literature of the field. It presents a manageable number of highly relevant sources on topics of interest to a wide range of researchers. The sources are scholarly, but also accessible to 'practitioners'."

– Lisa Stimatz, MLS, University of North Carolina at Chapel Hill, USA

"It is an excellent and well designed database which will facilitate research, publication, and teaching. It is a very useful tool to have."

– George Ditsa, PhD, University of Wollongong, Australia

"I have accessed the database and find it to be a valuable tool to the IT/IS community. I found valuable articles meeting my search criteria 95% of the time."

– Prof. Lynda Louis, Xavier University of Louisiana, USA

Recommended for use by researchers who wish to immediately download PDFs of individual chapters or articles.

www.igi-global.com/e-resources/infosci-ondemand

www.igi-global.com

Printed in the United States
By Bookmasters